Why Do You Need This New Edition?

If you're wondering why you should buy this new edition of *The Longman Pocket Writer's Companion*, here are seven good reasons!

❶ **A new Ten Serious Errors section** helps you recognize and correct major errors that make it hard for readers to understand your writing, including fragments, run-ons, unnecessary commas, and more.

❷ **A new chapter on Assessing Writing** (Ch. 10) offers you strategies for seeing your own writing objectively as well as tips for anticipating how others might evaluate your work.

❸ **A new chapter on Writing for General Education Courses** (Ch. 8) helps you analyze your college assignments. You'll also find tips to help you with the most common writing tasks across the General Education curriculum (such as writing summaries, annotated bibliographies, and essay exams), helping you to write more effectively in all your courses.

❹ **A new chapter on Writing in the Disciplines** (Ch. 9) will help you write papers common in the majors (such as interpretations, textual and visual analyses, abstracts, lab reports, and researched reports) to set you up for success as your college career progresses.

❺ **New documentation entries** illustrate how to cite sources such as blogs and podcasts, genres so new that they aren't covered in many texts.

❻ **New student sample pages in the CMS and CSE Style chapters** (Chs. 19, 20) ensure that you see sample student research writing in all four of the major academic documentation styles.

❼ **New Source Samples in the MLA and APA Style chapters** (Chs. 17, 18) show you where in the original source you can find all the information you need for citation.

THE
Longman Pocket Writer's Companion

THIRD EDITION

CHRIS M. ANSON
North Carolina State University

ROBERT A. SCHWEGLER
University of Rhode Island

MARCIA F. MUTH
University of Colorado at Denver

PEARSON
Longman

New York San Francisco Boston
London Toronto Sydney Tokyo Singapore Madrid
Mexico City Munich Paris Cape Town Hong Kong Montreal

Acquisitions Editor: Lauren A. Finn
Senior Supplements Editor: Donna Campion
Executive Marketing Manager: Megan Galvin-Fak
Production Manager: Bob Ginsberg
Project Coordination, Text Design, and Electronic Page Makeup:
    Nesbitt Graphics, Inc.
Cover Design Manager/Cover Designer: John Callahan
Visual Researcher: Rona Tuccillo
Senior Manufacturing Buyer: Alfred C. Dorsey
Printer and Binder: RR Donnelley & Sons Company/Crawfordsville
Cover Printer: Phoenix Color Corporation

For permission to use copyrighted material, grateful acknowledgment is made to the copyright holders on pp. vi and 265, which are hereby made part of this copyright page.

Library of Congress Cataloging-in-Publication Data

Anson, Christopher M., 1954-
  Longman pocket writer's companion / Chris M. Anson, Robert A. Schwegler,
Marcia F. Muth.-- 3rd ed.
        p. cm.
  Includes index.
  Includes bibliographical references and index.
  ISBN-13: 978-0-205-59142-8
  ISBN-10: 0-205-59142-6
 1. English language--Rhetoric--Handbooks, manuals, etc. 2. Report
writing--Handbooks, manuals, etc. I. Schwegler, Robert A. II. Muth, Marcia
F. III. Title.
  PE1408.A61846 2008
  808'.042--dc22

                                                      2007052457

Visit us at www.ablongman.com

ISBN-13: 978-0-205-59142-8
ISBN-10:   0-205-59142-6

1 2 3 4 5 6 7 8 9 10—DOC—11 10 09 08

Guide for Using This Handbook

When you're a busy writer in academic, work, and public communities, you want to make the most of your time. This book is designed to help you find what you need quickly and efficiently.

Strategy 1: Try the index at the end of the book. It includes key terms, subtopics, and related entries.

Strategy 2: Use the menu inside the front cover. This menu identifies sections and chapters so you can easily find main topics.

Strategy 3: Use the table of contents inside the back cover. Skim the contents to track down the chapter or topic you need. The chapter numbers and section letters noted there are used in cross-references and are easy to spot on the tabs on each page.

Strategy 4: Match editing symbols on your paper with corresponding sections of the text. Look inside the back cover for a list of common revising and editing symbols. Identify the marks on your paper, and turn to the relevant section of the text.

Strategy 5: Use the special features of the text.

- **Look for the "recognize and revise" approach.** Many chapters, especially those on grammar and usage, first introduce a problem using a Reader's Reaction and sample sentences. Then the chapter shows how to recognize and revise or edit the problem in your writing.

SERIOUS
ERROR
- **Review Ten Serious Errors.** This guide, beginning on page 225, explains how to recognize and revise ten major errors that confuse or irritate readers. If you find a sentence like yours, revise it, or turn to the chapter with further advice. Look for an icon like the one shown in the margin on the left to help you easily identify each section that discusses a serious error.

- **Apply the Strategies.** Each Strategy suggests how to apply general advice, recognize problems, or revise and edit your own writing.
- **Compare the examples with your own sentences.** Skim the draft sentences in the section that seems the most likely place to look for a problem. Find a sentence like your own. Read the explanation with it, and note any label so that you can learn how to recognize the problem. Use the revised or edited sentence as a pattern for your own changes.
- **Look for boldfaced terms.** These key terms are explained right in the text. Turn also to the Glossary on page 233 for more terms and usage matters.
- **Find the ESL Advice.** If you are not a native speaker of English, use the Guide to ESL Advice (p. 265). It lists the ESL Advice integrated in the text.
- **Look for charts and boxes.** They make information easy to spot.
- **Turn to sample documents.** Selections from sample research papers conclude the chapters (17–20) on all four styles for documenting sources. They show how other students have presented their papers. Sample documents in 6e also show how you might design a paper, résumé, or newsletter project.

Credits

Page 1: Lopez, Barry, "About This Life." New York, NY: Knopf, 1998. **Page 11:** Sankey, Jay, "Zen & the Art of Stand-up Comedy." New York, NY: Routledge/Taylor & Francis Books, Inc., 1998. **Page 19:** AFP/Getty Images. **Page 21:** The Daily Moose Newsletter. Reprinted by Permission. Photo courtesy of LetsGoSeeIt.com. **Page 39:** First two sentences on page 39 from Part 2, "Conducting Research" from "Dust Tracks on a Road" by Zora Neale Hurston. Copyright 1942 by Zora Neale Hurston, renewed 1970 by John C. Hurston. Reprinted by permission of HarperCollins Publishers. **Pages 52–53:** Reisberg, Leo, "Colleges Step Up Efforts to Combat Alcohol Abuse," *The Chronicle of Higher Education*, June 12, 1998, Vol. 44, No. 40. **Page 54:** Tucker, Larry A., "Effect of Weight Training on Self-Concept: A Profile of Those Influenced Most," *Research Quarterly for Exercise & Sport*, 1983. **Pages 57–60:** Mathieu, Paula, & Ken McAllister, "Questions for Evaluating Web Sources," CRITT Web Site (Critical Resources in Teaching with Technology), 1998. http://www.engl.uic.edu/~stp/. **Page 58:** "Got Latte?" Screen shot used by permission of the California Milk Processor Board. **Page 59:** "Lactose Intolerance." Screen shot from National Digestive Diseases Information Clearinghouse, National Institutes of Health, http://digestive.niddk.nih.gov/ddiseases/pubs/lactoseintolerance. **Pages 61–62:** Garrett, Laurie, "The Coming Plague." New York, NY: Penguin Books, 1994. **Page 65:** Hall, Donald, excerpt from "The Black-Faced Sheep" from *Old and New Poems*. Copyright © 1990 by Donald Hall. Reprinted by permission of Houghton Mifflin Company. All rights reserved. **Page 67:** Gibaldi, Joseph, *MLA Handbook for Writers of Research Papers*. Modern Language Association, 2003. **Page 67:** From *Publication Manual of the American Psychological Association*, 5th ed., p xxiii. APA, 2001. **Page 71:** Bright, Michael, *Animal Language*. Ithaca, NY: Cornell University Press, 1984. **Page 72:** Honey, Maureen, *Creating Rosie the Riveter*. Amherst, MA: University of Massachusetts Press, 1984. **Page 72:** Committee of Concerned Journalists, "A Statement of Concern," *The Media & Morality*. Ed. Robert M. Baird, William E. Loges, & Stuart E. Rosenbaum. New York, NY: Prometheus Books, 1999. **Page 73:** Twain, Mark. *Huckleberry Finn*. New York, NY: HarperCollins Publishers, 1998. **Page 75:** Hand, Wayland D., "Folk Medical Magic and Symbolism in the West," *Magic, Witchcraft and Religion: An Anthropological Study of the Supernatural*, 3rd ed. Ed. Arthur C. Lehmann & James Myers. Mayfield Publishing, 1993. **Pages 75–76:** Gmelch, George, "Baseball Magic." *Transaction*, 1971. **Page 91:** Screen shot of search results in html format from Blackwell

(Credits continue on p. 265)

PART

1 Writing and Reading

Voices
from the Community

"Every story is an act of trust between a writer and a reader; each story, in the end, is social. Whatever a writer sets down can harm or help the community of which he or she is a part."

—Barry Lopez, "A Voice," *About This Life:*
Journeys on the Threshold of Memory

1 | Writing and Reading in Communities

Writing depends on the relationship between writers and readers. Whether you are drafting a history paper, a memo at work, or a neighborhood flyer, try to envision the **community of readers and writers** you are addressing—people with shared, though not necessarily identical, interests, goals, and preferences. Their expectations help you decide how best to shape ideas, information, and experiences you want to share with them.

Participating in academic, work, and public communities means talking, reading, and especially writing. These broad communities share some preferences—such as favoring clear, specific writing—and differ on others, such as addressing the reader as *you*. Understanding such preferences can help you recognize readers' expectations as well as writers' choices.

1a Understanding your writing situation

Begin by "reading" your situation, often a specific assignment or project.

- What is your purpose? What do you want or need to achieve?
- How will you relate to readers? What will they expect?
- What is your subject? What do you know, or need to know, about it?

> **STRATEGY** Pinpoint your writing task.
>
> Look over your task or assignment. Draw a straight line under words (usually nouns) that specify a **topic.** Put a wavy line under action words (verbs) that tell what your writing needs to *do*, its **purpose.**
>
> **Assignment:** Analyze a magazine ad for hidden cultural assumptions. Describe what happens in the ad, noting camera angle, color, and focus.

THREE COMMUNITIES OF READERS AND WRITERS			
	ACADEMIC	**PUBLIC**	**WORK**
GOALS	Create or exchange knowledge	Persuade, participate, inform	Solve problems, inform, promote
FORMS	Analysis, interpretation, lab report, proposal, article, bibliography	Letter, flyer, newsletter, position paper, fact sheet	Memo, letter, ad, report, minutes, proposal, instructions
WRITING CHARACTERISTICS	Reasoning, analysis, insights, evidence, detail, fair exploration	Advocacy, evidence, shared values, recognition of others	Clarity, accuracy, conciseness, focus on problem

Whatever your task and whatever your broad community (academic, public, or work), you need to address your specific readers, actual or potential. Always ask, Exactly what do my readers expect?

STRATEGY **Analyze your readers.**

Who. How large is your audience? How well do you know them? Are they close or distant?

Expectations. What do typical readers expect in your community?

Knowledge. What are your readers likely to know about your topic? What do they want or need to know?

Background. What defines your readers socially, culturally, or educationally? How do they think?

Relationships. Are your readers peers or superiors? What do they expect you to do? What do you expect them to do?

1b Moving from reading to writing

Good writing is often inspired by what others have written. Critical reading will help you respond to a text by developing your own insights.

Reading critically. **Critical reading** leads to analysis and interpretation. Before reading, review the table of contents, abstract, or headings. Scan the text for key ideas and concepts. Note any information about the author, intended audience, or occasion for which the text was written.

• Skim each section after you have read it, reviewing major points and their connections.
• Note what you have learned and what you find puzzling or confusing. Reread later to clarify your understanding.
• Sum up or restate the text's main points or ideas in your own words.
• List the major insights, opinions, or ideas.

> **STRATEGY**   **Interact with a text to develop insights.**
>
> • **Question.** What do you want or need to know?
> • **Synthesize.** How does the text relate to other texts or other views? What other views does it acknowledge (or fail to anticipate)?
> • **Interpret.** What does the writer mean or imply? What do you conclude about the text's outlook or bias?
> • **Assess.** How do you evaluate its value and accuracy?

Turning reading into writing.   Try putting your responses to a text into informal writing that you can later develop into essays or reports.

• **Marginal comments.** In the margins of a text (if it belongs to you) or a photocopy, write your interpretations, questions, objections, or evaluations (for a class, service project, civic activity, or work task).
• **Journal entries.** In a journal or on note cards, respond to your reading, noting what you think or where you agree or disagree with the author.

1c Paying attention to the writing process

Experienced writers know that paying attention to all parts of the writing process generally leads to more effective writing.

Discovering and planning. To identify and develop a promising topic, use techniques such as these.

- **Freewrite** quickly by hand or at the computer for five or ten minutes. Don't stop; just slip into engaging ideas.
- Try **focused freewriting,** exploring a specific idea.
- Ask **strategic questions** to stir memories and suggest what to gather. Begin with *what, why,* and *why not.* Next try *who, where, when, how.*
- Use **interactive prompts** from the Web, computer lab, tutoring center, or your software.

To focus and organize your drafting, try the following strategies.

- Try **clustering.** Write an idea at the center of a page, and then jot down random associations. Circle key ideas; add lines to connect them.
- **List ideas and details** you want to discuss.
- **Chunk** related points and material in files (by topic or section).
- Consider a **formal outline** (numbered and lettered sections) or a **working outline** (introduction, body, conclusion) to order points.

Drafting. Begin drafting once you have a main idea (or **thesis,** see 2a) and a general structure. Draft quickly; don't worry about perfect sentences. Or try **semidrafting,** writing until you stall out, noting *etc.* or a list instead of full text, and moving on to the next point.

Revising, editing, proofreading. Revision means critically *reading* and *reworking.* It precedes **editing** to fine-tune and **proofreading** to spot errors.

REVISING, EDITING, AND PROOFREADING

Major revision. Redraft passages, reorganize, add, and delete.
Minor revision. Rework illogical, wordy, or weak passages.
Collaborative revision. Ask peers to suggest improvements.

Editing. Improve clarity, style, and economy; check grammar, sentence structure, wording, punctuation, and mechanics.

Proofreading. Focus on details and final appearance, especially spelling, punctuation, and typing errors.

2 | Developing a Thesis

Most writing needs a clear **thesis**—a main idea, insight, or opinion that you wish to share. Announcing it in a **thesis statement** helps readers follow your reasoning and helps you organize and maintain focus.

2a Creating a thesis statement

To guide readers, you may state your thesis after introducing your topic and its background. Begin with a **rough thesis,** a sentence (or two) that identifies your perspective and states your assertion or conclusion.

VAGUE TOPIC	Ritalin
STILL A TOPIC	The use of Ritalin for kids
STILL A TOPIC (NO ASSERTION)	Problems of Ritalin for kids with attention-deficit disorder (ADD)
	READER'S REACTION: But what should parents do?
ROUGH THESIS (ASSERTION)	Parents should be careful about Ritalin for kids with ADD.

Extend a rough thesis, making it more precise and complex. For example, what stance should parents take: Avoid Ritalin? Use it cautiously?

EXTENDED THESIS   Although Ritalin is widely used to treat children with ADD, parents should explore both their child's problem and all treatment options before relying on it.

STRATEGY **Sharpen your thesis until your final draft.**

Treat your thesis as tentative. Refine it to offer a clear assertion—focused, limited, yet complex enough to warrant readers' attention.

2b Designing an appropriate thesis

Refine your thesis to suit your purpose or your readers.

General thesis. Readers will expect your conclusions or perspectives.

> Sooner or later, teenagers stop listening to parents and turn to each other for advice, sometimes with disastrous results.

Informative thesis. Readers will expect to learn why this information is of interest and how you'll organize it.

> When students search for online advice about financial aid, they can find help at three very different kinds of Web sites.

Argumentative thesis. Readers will expect to find your opinion, perhaps with other views on the issue, too.

> Although bioengineered crops may pose some dangers, their potential for combating worldwide hunger justifies their careful use.

Academic thesis. Readers will expect you to state your specific conclusion and a plan to support it according to the field's criteria.

> My survey of wedding announcements in local newspapers from 1960 to 2000 shows that religious background and ethnicity have decreased in importance as factors in mate selection.

3 Providing Support and Reasoning Clearly

Whether exploring an academic topic, making a recommendation at work, or advocating a stand on an issue, the path your thinking takes is called a **chain of reasoning.** Readers will find your writing logical and convincing if it provides support suitable for the subject, purpose, and community.

CRITICAL REASONING IN THREE MAJOR COMMUNITIES			
	ACADEMIC	**PUBLIC**	**WORK**
GOAL	Analysis of text, phenom- enon, or creative work to interpret or explain	Participation in demo- cratic processes to con- tribute, inform, or per- suade	Analysis of problems to supply information and propose solutions
REASONING PROCESS	Detailed reasoning leading to specific conclusions	Plausible reasoning to support own view without ranting	Accurate analysis of problem or need with clear solution
EVIDENCE	Specific references to detailed evidence, with citations of others' work	Relevant evidence, often local, to sub- stantiate views and probabilities	Sufficient evidence to show the problem's importance and justify a solution
EXAMPLE	Present new expla- nation of Alzheimer's	Propose community facility for patients	Describe marketing strategy for Alzheimer's drug

3a Reasoning critically

What processes support critical reasoning?

- Exploring a question, problem, or experience
- Uniting ideas and information to reach a conclusion

- Focusing on the end point of the chain of reasoning—the main conclusion (often your thesis statement)

TYPES OF CONCLUSIONS YOU MIGHT DRAW

Interpretations of meaning (experience, literature, film), importance (current event, history), or causes and effects (problem, event)

Analyses of elements (problem, situation, phenomenon, subject)

Propositions about an issue, problem, or policy

Judgments about "right" or "wrong" (action, policy), quality (creative work, performance), or effectiveness (solution, course of action)

Recommendations for guidelines, policies, or responses

Warnings about consequences of action or inaction

STRATEGY **Focus on your conclusions.**

List all your conclusions, interpretations, or opinions. What others come to mind? Which are main and which secondary? What explanation or evidence connects these points? Does each lead logically to the next?

3b Providing support

A convincing chain of reasoning gives readers information that supports generalizations. **Information** includes facts of all kinds—examples, data, details, quotations—that you present as reliable, confirmable, or generally undisputed. **Generalizations** are conclusions based on and supported by information. Information turns into **evidence** when it's used to persuade a reader that an idea is reasonable (see 7c).

TYPES OF EVIDENCE

Examples of an event, idea, person, place, object, image, or text, brief or extended, from personal experience or research

Details of an idea, place, situation, or phenomenon

Information about times, places, participants, numbers, consequences, surroundings, and relationships

Statistics, perhaps presented in tables or charts

Background on context, history, or effects

Quotations from experts, participants, or other writers

3c Evaluating support

Assess evidence critically. How **abundant** is it? Is it **sufficient** to support your conclusions? Is it **relevant, accurate,** and **well documented?**

STRATEGY Align your evidence with your thesis.

General thesis. Supply evidence that fits your claim and readers' expectations: statistics, interviews, examples from experience.

Informative thesis. Give evidence showing a subject's elements.

Argumentative thesis. Supply information, examples, and quotations to support your stand, answer objections, and refute opposing views.

Academic thesis. Provide evidence that meets the discipline's standards; cite contributions of others.

4 | Paragraphing for Readers

Every time you indent to begin a new paragraph, you signal academic, public, or workplace readers to watch for a shift in topic or emphasis.

4a Focusing paragraphs

A **focused paragraph** has a clear topic and a main idea that guide readers through the specifics of your discussion. Help readers recognize the focus by stating your topic and main idea or perspective in a **topic sentence.** Place this sentence at a paragraph's end, leave it unstated but clearly implied, or add a clarifying sentence to explain further. When you want readers to grasp the point right away, put this sentence first.

<u>When writing jokes, it's a good idea to avoid vague generalizations.</u> Don't just talk about "fruit" when you can talk about "an apple." Strong writing creates a single image for everyone in the crowd, each person imagining a very similar thing. But when you say "fruit," people are either imagining several different kinds of fruit or they aren't really thinking of anything in particular, and both things can significantly reduce their emotional investment in the joke. But when you say "an apple," everyone has *a clear picture,* and thus a feeling.

—Jay Sankey, "Zen and the Art of Stand-Up Comedy"

> **STRATEGY** **Check your paragraph focus.**
> - What is your main point in this paragraph?
> - How many different ideas does it cover?
> - Does it elaborate on the main idea? Do details fit?
> - Have you announced your focus to readers? Where?

4b Making paragraphs coherent

A paragraph is **coherent** if each sentence leads clearly to the next, forming an easy-to-understand arrangement. When sentences are out of logical order or jump abruptly, readers may struggle to follow the thought. Use key words to keep readers aware of the arrangement of ideas.

People married for a long time often develop similar **facial features. Younger couples** display only chance resemblances between their **faces.**

Because **they** share emotions for many years, however, **older couples** acquire similar **expressions.**

STRATEGY   **Check your paragraph coherence.**

- Does the paragraph repeat key words and synonyms naming the topic and main points? Do these words begin or end sentences, or are they buried in the middle?
- Are ideas arranged logically? What transitions relate sentences?
- What parallel structures emphasize similar ideas? (See 30a–b.)

USEFUL TRANSITIONS FOR SHOWING RELATIONSHIPS

Time and sequence: next, later, after, meanwhile, earlier, first, second, shortly, subsequently, soon, since, finally, last, as long as, at that time

Comparison: likewise, similarly, also, again, in comparison

Contrast: in contrast, on the one hand . . . on the other hand, however, although, yet, but, nevertheless, at the same time, regardless

Examples: for example, for instance, such as, thus, namely, specifically

Cause and effect: as a result, consequently, due to, for this reason, accordingly, if . . . then, as a consequence, because of

Place: next to, above, behind, beyond, between, here, there, opposite, to the right, in the background, over, under

Addition: and, too, moreover, in addition, besides, next, also, finally

Concession: of course, naturally, granted, it is true that, certainly

Conclusion: in conclusion, as a result, as the data show

Repetition: in other words, once again, to repeat

Summary: on the whole, to sum up, in short, therefore

4c Developing paragraphs

Paragraph development provides the informative examples, facts, details, explanations, or arguments readers expect to support a conclusion.

UNDERDEVELOPED

Recycling is always a good idea—or almost always. Recycling some products, even paper, may require more energy from fossil fuels and more valuable natural resources than making them the first time.

READER'S REACTION: I need to know more before I agree. Which products? How much energy does recycling take? What resources are consumed?

STRATEGY **Check your paragraph development.**

Highlight the material that develops your paragraph. Do you present enough to *inform* readers? Do you adequately *support* generalizations?

PATTERNS FOR PARAGRAPH DEVELOPMENT

Narrate: tell a story or anecdote; recreate events

Describe: provide detail about a scene, object, character, or feeling

Compare and contrast: explore similarities or differences; evaluate options

Explain a process: provide directions; tell how a mechanism, procedure, or natural process operates

Divide: separate into parts; explore their relationships

Classify: sort into groups; explain their relationships

Define: explain a term; illustrate a concept

Analyze causes and effects: consider why something happens

5 Matching Style and Strategy to a Community of Readers

Should you use *I* or *we*—or *you*? Should you add technical terms? Such choices depend less on your "voice" than on **community style**—preferences taken for granted by communities of readers and writers.

5a Recognizing a community's style

Consider the following to help you understand your options as a writer.

Formality. Do readers expect writing that is formal, complicated, and technical or relaxed and direct?

STYLE IN THREE MAJOR COMMUNITIES			
	ACADEMIC	**PUBLIC**	**WORK**
FORMALITY	Formality supports analytical approach and values of the field	Informality reveals personal involvement with serious issues	Informality reflects teamwork; formality shows respect
WRITER'S STANCE	Observer (*he, she, it*) or participant (*I, we*)	Involved person (*I, you*) or representative (*we, you*)	Team member (*we*) with personal concern (*I, you*)
LANGUAGE	Technical terms and methods of the field	Lively and emotional; few technical terms and little slang	Plain or technical terms but little vivid, figurative wording
DISTANCE	Objective and dispassionate, not personal or emotional	Passionate and personal about cause, issue, or group	Supportive, committed closeness with mutual respect
EXAMPLE	Presentation of data and findings	Pamphlet encouraging people to recycle	Instructions for new marketing campaign

	ACADEMIC	PUBLIC	WORK
EXPECTATIONS IN THREE MAJOR COMMUNITIES			
TYPICAL EXPECTATIONS OF READERS	Analyze or interpret a text or an event. Review and cite theory and research. Report original research findings. Reason logically about a question. Present your fresh insights.	Supply information about an issue, especially local background, data, and evidence. Encourage civic involvement and decision making. Persuade others to support a cause.	Provide or request information. Analyze problems. Recommend actions or solutions. Identify and evaluate alternatives.
TYPICAL STRATEGIES OF WRITERS	State your thesis and main points directly. Use detail to support your views. Write clearly and logically even on a complex topic. Acknowledge other views.	Persuade, enlighten, or energize readers through advocacy. Promote policies, actions, or solutions. Supply supporting evidence. Recognize interests of others.	Focus on the task, problem, or goal. Present matters accurately. Organize and summarize for busy readers. Use concise, clear, direct prose.

Writer's stance. How do writers identify themselves, readers, and the topic: *I, we, you, he, she, it, they?*

Language. What **diction**—word choices—do readers favor: vivid or neutral phrases, logical or informal links, technical or everyday terms?

Distance. Is a writer typically distant or involved, an insider or outsider, a participant or an observer?

5b Adjusting to a community's style

Examine your community's style as you read typical texts. For example, academic writers often analyze as distant observers using a field's terms and methods. They may use *I,* depending on the field, but seldom address readers directly. In contrast, work communities share values such as efficiency, often using *we* to build teamwork. In public exchanges, writers may be individual (*I*) or collective (*we*) partisans.

5c Recognizing a community's expectations

Your writing strategies should consider your audience's expectations. (See the box on p. 15.)

6 | Designing Documents for Readers

What makes your research report, essay, or letter memorable—clear, persuasive, and easy to read? The answer often lies in document design, considering the look of the page or screen and the processes of readers.

6a Planning your document

To design effective documents, sketch sample pages containing design features, or prepare a list of specifications that answers these questions.

- What kind of document or page format do my readers expect?
- How will I highlight the organization? Will I provide a table of contents?
- What font, typeface, and type size will I use?
- Will I integrate visual aids? Which ones? Will I use color?
- What are the copyright or legal issues when using others' materials?

6b Laying out your document

Layout is the arrangement of words, sentences, lists, and visuals on a printed page or screen. Supply visual cues, but don't overwhelm your text.

STRATEGY **Highlight to direct the reader's eye.**

- Use **boldface,** *italics,* shading, rules, and boxes to signal distinctions.
- Set off items in lists with numbers, letters, or bullets.
- Use CAPITALS, exclamation points (!!), and other cues sparingly for emphasis. Limit underlining (especially in Web pages with links).
- Use color to meet goals (such as warning), prioritize, trace a theme or sequence, or code symbols.
- Leave **white space**—open space not filled by other design elements— to break dense text into chunks.

Headings are phrases that forecast content or structure. Often larger and darker, they catch a reader's eye and lead to information.

STRATEGY **Design useful headings.**

- Orient headings specifically to your task or readers: **Deducting Student Loan Interest,** not **Student Loans.**
- Position headings uniformly (for example, center main headings but begin subheadings at the left margin).
- Add white space between headings and text, but not too much.
- Define heading levels consistently with visual features (font, style, position such as left margin or centered).
- Keep the wording of each level of heading parallel whenever possible.

6c Using type features

Consider readers' expectations as you judiciously use software options.

Type size. Both 10- and 12-point type are easy to read; the latter is most common in academic papers. Save sizes above 12 points for visuals.

8 point   10 point   12 point   16 point

Typefaces. Serif fonts have "little feet," small strokes at the end of each letter-form. Sans serif fonts lack them. Readers find serif type easier to read in text while sans serif works well in titles, headings, labels, and material onscreen. Reserve decorative fonts for brochures, invitations, or posters.

N **Serif**   N **Sans serif**

6d Using visuals

Drawings, diagrams, and photographs can speed communication. **Tables** order text or numbers in columns and rows. **Graphs** rely on two labeled axes (vertical and horizontal), using lines or bars to relate variables. **Pie charts** show percentages of a whole.

> **STRATEGY** Integrate visuals with text.
> - Choose simple visual aids that make a point; avoid decorative filler.
> - Place a visual near related text, and refer to it in the text.
> - Label all graphics as figures (except for tables), number them, and supply short, accurate captions. (See 16e–f.)
> - Credit sources for all borrowed graphics, and respect copyright.

6e Sample documents

The following samples show document design in action.

Sample Academic Paper with Illustration, MLA Format

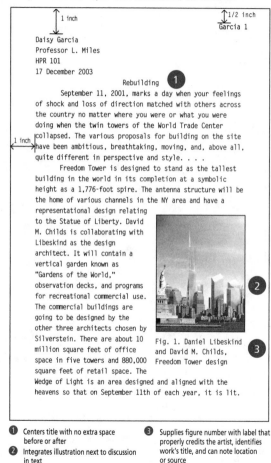

↑ 1 inch

↑ 1/2 inch
Garcia 1

Daisy Garcia
Professor L. Miles
HPR 101
17 December 2003

Rebuilding ❶

September 11, 2001, marks a day when your feelings of shock and loss of direction matched with others across the country no matter where you were or what you were doing when the twin towers of the World Trade Center collapsed. The various proposals for building on the site have been ambitious, breathtaking, moving, and, above all, quite different in perspective and style. . . .

Freedom Tower is designed to stand as the tallest building in the world in its completion at a symbolic height as a 1,776-foot spire. The antenna structure will be the home of various channels in the NY area and have a representational design relating to the Statue of Liberty. David M. Childs is collaborating with Libeskind as the design architect. It will contain a vertical garden known as "Gardens of the World," observation decks, and programs for recreational commercial use. The commercial buildings are going to be designed by the other three architects chosen by Silverstein. There are about 10 million square feet of office space in five towers and 880,000 square feet of retail space. The Wedge of Light is an area designed and aligned with the heavens so that on September 11th of each year, it is lit.

❷

Fig. 1. Daniel Libeskind and David M. Childs, Freedom Tower design ❸

1 inch (left margin marker)

❶ Centers title with no extra space before or after

❷ Integrates illustration next to discussion in text

❸ Supplies figure number with label that properly credits the artist, identifies work's title, and can note location or source

Sample Workplace Résumé

Tammy Jo Helton
550 Sundown Ct., Dayton, OH 45427
453-555-5555   TJ@mailnow.com

CERTIFICATION
Elementary Education (grades 1-8)
Bachelor of Arts, August 2007, Wright State University, Dayton, OH

EDUCATION
Wright State University, 2004-2007, College of Education
Sinclair Community College, 2003-2004, general education
Wayne High School, 2002 graduate, college preparatory

AWARDS
Phi Kappa Phi National Honor Society 2006, 2007
Dean's list 2005, 2006, 2007

TEACHING EXPERIENCE

Student Teaching
Seventh grade physical science, L.T. Ball Junior High, Tipp City, OH
Planned and implemented lessons while maintaining classroom control.

Observation
Shilohview, Trotwood, OH
Implemented preplanned lessons.

Teaching
Sixth grade religious education class, Dayton, OH
Currently responsible for planning and implementing lessons.

WORK EXPERIENCE
Goal Line Sports Grill, 2004-present: Server, cash register, supervisor
Frisch's Big Boy, 2002-2004: Server, inventory, preparation
Shilohview Park, 2001-2003: Park Counselor, activity planner

INTERESTS AND ACTIVITIES
Took dance lessons for ten years; played drums in the school band.

References available on request.

1. Centers name, address, phone, and email address
2. Uses capitals for main headings
3. Separates page into sections using white space
4. Uses short lines for compressed information
5. Uses reverse chronological order.

Sample Student Project

Thursday
July 8th, 2003

Volume XX
Issue 2

The Daily Moose

North America's Only Newspaper Devoted to Moose Lovers Everywhere. Twenty-Two Years and Growing.

❷

Big Moose Comes From Small Dreams

❶

Staff Reporter: Andrea White

Growing up, your favorite animal may have been a cat, dog, or turtle. Even as exotic as parrots, giraffes and elephants. But in areas north of Chicago and Boston, children wish for pets like deer, caribou and even moose. Moose usually occupy areas in the northern United States and Canada, finding them in southern California is quite unusual. However, traveling to Orange County, California you might see dozens, even hundreds of these winter-weather giants. Mainly Seconds, a craft/antique store in Orange County, has a display of numerous moose paraphernalia all collected by the "Moose" himself, Mike Bonk.

In 1982, Mike's first store opened and received a gift from his wife and former employees. It was a corduroy moose head with a plaque inscribed, "The Moose is Loose". This present hangs on the wall near the entrance next to painted words, *The Moose Museum*. The museum started when Mike put his personal items on display around the store. It seemed that as the store increased and prospered, his collection did also. Soon there was so much moose collectibles; it formed itself into a museum.

❸

The Moose Museum Located at Mainly Seconds,

This museum is not like any other. Set in the back section of the store, it consists of about fifty cases and 10 aisles of various products either resembling or being moose associated. "If it's moose, it's in here" Mike said during a recent interview. And it's true (Cont. on page 2).

The Moose Museum
Cordially Invites You …

❺

To Explore the Wide
World of Moose

Come experience the
Northern Wilderness in
Sunny California.
New Exhibits! More Moose!

789 S. Tustin Avenue   555-9876

❹ ## Warning: Moose X-ing

Travel columnist: Caroline Cesserta

My family and I always agonize about where to travel for our yearly summer vacation. This year, my daughter and I agreed on a nice mountain lodge in Colorado while my husband and other daughter sided on a tropical getaway to Mexico. To compromise, we decided to tour California starting from the Mexican border up to Oregon. One of my personal favorite spots is very unusual store I discovered when we were stopped at a rest stop and someone noticed my moose decal on the back window. (Cont. Pg. 2)

❶ Selects varied typefaces and sizes for a system of headings
❷ Uses single column for lead story
❸ Integrates photograph and text
❹ Uses double column for additional text
❺ Encloses highlighted text in oval "box"

7 | Constructing an Argument

In argumentative writing, you present and endorse an outlook, opinion, or course of action. You persuade by focusing on reasons, evidence, and values to encourage readers to agree with your opinion or proposal.

7a Identifying an issue

At the heart of argumentative writing is an **issue**—a topic about which readers recognize two (or more) clearly differing, worthwhile opinions. Many arguments address **existing issues,** ongoing disagreements about broad issues (gun control or global warming) or specific concerns (a new campus drinking policy or local limits on development). To identify **potential issues,** try evaluating consequences of a policy or questioning what is taken for granted ("Do hybrid cars always save energy?") or widely believed (*Opinion:* Early decision programs benefit college applicants. *Response:* Do they?).

ISSUES IN THREE COMMUNITIES			
	ACADEMIC	**PUBLIC**	**WORK**
GENERAL	Standardized testing Affirmative action in college admissions	Genetically altered foods Violence and sex on television	Child care at work Ethnically targeted marketing
LOCAL	Housing regulations at Nontanko River U	A local crusade against a television series	Discipline policies at Abtech's ChildCare

7b Developing an argumentative thesis

To argue effectively, you need to identify your own opinion (your **claim**) and communicate it to readers in an **argumentative thesis statement.**

Explore your perspective. First articulate your opinion to yourself to focus your ideas, values, and feelings. Write informally about your intuitive reactions, whether scorn, pity, fear, or outrage. List your strongest concerns, and sum up your responses. Identify facts, examples, and ideas that support your opinions. Then think about objections, and list them too.

Focus and revise your claim. Limit your argument by identifying a specific claim and its purpose. Do you want to argue that an activity or belief is good or bad? If so, you are asking readers to agree with a **value judgment.** Do you want them to support a course of action? If so, you are asking them to agree with a **policy.** Do you want them to agree with an explanation? If so, you are asking them to endorse an **interpretation.**

> **STRATEGY**   State and revise your claim in memos to yourself.
>
> To: Self
>
> I find using roadblocks to catch drunk drivers really disturbing. We need to keep drunks off the road, but this remedy is extreme. I want readers to agree that roadblocks violate civil liberties and should be banned.

Revise your claim to reflect what you discover through your research. Then write yourself a second memo.

Create (and revise) a thesis statement. An explicit thesis makes your claim clear to readers and helps them follow your reasoning.

1. Identify a specific issue and your opinion.
2. Provide a clear and logical statement of your argumentative claim.

3. Suggest a general direction for your argument.
4. Indicate related claims or opinions.

STRATEGY Revise your thesis statement.

- **State your thesis** in a sentence (or two), using sentence patterns like "X should be altered/banned/approved because . . ."; "I propose this plan/policy/action because . . ."; or "Y is beneficial/ineffective/harmful because. . . ."
- **Check your tentative thesis** to see whether it blurs your specific purposes for arguing or makes illogical assumptions.

BLURRED AND ILLOGICAL : Police should stop conducting unconstitutional roadblocks and substitute more frequent visual checks of erratic driving to identify people who are driving while intoxicated.

- **Revise to focus** your thesis on a clear issue, a single claim, or two related claims you will argue in appropriate order.

SINGLE PROPOSITIONS : Roadblocks used to identify drunk drivers are unconstitutional because they violate important civil liberties.

Frequent visual checks for erratic driving can effectively identify intoxicated drivers.

7c Developing reasons and supporting evidence

To encourage readers to agree with your argumentative claim, you need to give them a series of reasons, each followed by evidence.

TENTATIVE THESIS : Coursework for certification should continue after people start teaching because this efficient approach can increase the number of dedicated new teachers.

REASON 1 : People learn a skill or activity best while doing it.
EVIDENCE: **comparisons to medical internships and residencies; reports on innovative teacher training**

REASON 2   Practicing teachers are often more motivated learners than
                  are pre-service teachers.

> **EVIDENCE: information from scholarly article comparing responses of participants in pre- and in-service courses**

REASON 3   New teachers will succeed in their first jobs, especially if
(COUNTER-   their schools supervise and support them.
ARGUMENT)

Varied evidence can help develop your reasons effectively (see 3b).

- Logically justify your opinions and reasoning.
- Encourage readers to trust your conclusions and proposals, understand
  your reasoning, and connect it with their experiences.
- Help readers envision a proposed action or a new policy.

Examples from your own or others' experience can support a claim and
draw readers to your point of view as can quotations and ideas from authorities. Detailed information may include statistics, technical features, results
of surveys and interviews, and historical background. Visual evidence can
highlight points and appeal to values and emotions either as facts and statistics in graphs, tables, or other figures or as photographs or drawings that
are evidence in themselves.

7d Presenting counterarguments

Traditional argument is like a battle: you imagine someone who disagrees with
you and then try to undermine that adversary's points or **counterarguments.**
In contemporary argument, you acknowledge alternative views, not so much
to win as to convince others of the validity of your views.

STRATEGY   Develop counterarguments.

Divide a sheet of paper into three columns. On the left, list the main points
supporting your opinion. Write opposing points in the middle column as
if you oppose your original stance. On the right, list possible defenses for the
counterarguments. Note any sources that would support your argument.

7e Reasoning logically

Effective argument assembles your opinions and supporting evidence in an order that reflects a chain of reasoning and avoids flaws in logic.

- **Reasoning from consequences.** You argue for or against an action or outlook, based on real or likely consequences, good or bad.
- **Reasoning from comparisons.** You argue for or against a policy or point of view based on similar situations, problems, or actions.
- **Reasoning from authority and testimony.** You draw evidence from recognized experts or from people with relevant experience.
- **Reasoning from examples and statistics.** You draw on events, situations, and problems presented as illustrations or as statistics.

Data-warrant-claim reasoning. The philosopher Stephen Toulmin identifies kinds of statements reasonable people make when they argue: *data* correspond to evidence, *claims* to the conclusion, and *warrants* to a reader's mental process connecting data to claim, answering "How?"

Suppose you are examining the safety of cars. As data, you have a study on the odds of injury in different models of cars. To argue effectively, you need to show readers *how* the data and your claim are connected, what patterns (probable facts—warrants) link data and claim.

DATA
Ratings of each car model show likelihood of injury (scale: 1–10).

CLAIM
For the average consumer, buying a large car is a good way to reduce the likelihood of being injured in an accident.

WARRANT
- The cars in the ratings fall into three easily recognized groups: small, medium, large. (probable fact)
- The large cars as a group have a lower average likelihood of injury to passengers than either of the other groups. (probable fact)
- Although some other cars have low likelihood of injury, almost all the large cars seem safe. (assertion + probable fact)

- Few consumers will go over the crash ratings to see which models get good or poor scores. (assertion)

Logical and emotional appeals. Logical and emotional appeals can enhance your credibility as a writer if you arrange your reasons and evidence in ways that most people will accept as reasonable. Emotional strategies focus on the values and beliefs of readers that motivate them to care about an issue. However, such appeals work best when they are also supported by logical strategies—reasoning based on likely good or bad consequences, relevant comparisons, authoritative experts, trustworthy testimony, pertinent illustrations, and statistics. As you evaluate your evidence and shape your argument, watch for **logical fallacies** (flaws in reasoning) that take some common forms.

- **Faulty Cause-and-Effect Relationship** (*post hoc, ergo propter hoc,* "after this, therefore because of this"): attempts to persuade you that because one event follows another, the first causes the second.

  The increase in violence on television is making the crime rate soar.
  READER'S REACTION: **This may be true, but no evidence here links the two.**

- **False Analogy:** compares two things that seem, but aren't, comparable.

  Raising the speed limit is like offering free cocktails at a meeting of recovering alcoholics.
  READER'S REACTION: **I don't see the connection. Most drivers aren't recovering from an addiction to high-speed driving.**

- **Red Herring:** distracts readers from the real argument.

  Gun control laws will decrease domestic violence and accidents. People opposed to gun control are probably criminals themselves.
  READER'S REACTION: **The second sentence doesn't follow logically or add support. It's just a distracting attack on people who disagree.**

- **Ad Hominem:** attacks the person, not the issue.

  Of course Walt Smith would support a bill to aid farmers—he owns several farms in the Midwest.
  READER'S REACTION: **I'd like to hear reactions to his ideas, please.**

- **Begging the Question:** presents assumptions as facts.

    Most people try to be physically fit; obviously, they fear getting old.
    READER'S REACTION: **I don't see any evidence that people fear aging—or that they are working on their physical fitness, either.**

- **Circular Reasoning:** supports an assertion with the assertion itself.

    The university should increase funding of intramural sports because it has a responsibility to back its sports programs financially.
    READER'S REACTION: **So the university should fund sports because it should fund sports?**

8 | Writing for General Education Courses

When you sign up for a 100-level class—a general education course—you may be asked to weigh two sides of an issue, to analyze what something is or why it happens, or to sum up the ideas in a reading.

8a General academic writing assignments

Suppose that your first paper for Art 100: Introduction to Art History is due soon, based on this assignment. How can you figure out what to do?

NAME OF TASK	**Short interpretive paper:** Locate a piece of art from the
REQUIRED SUBJECT AND APPROACH	period we are studying. Using the concepts covered in class, write an interpretation of the work based on its characteristics.
KEY WORDS	*Identify* the work and the artist, but *focus* on the art, not on the
AUDIENCE	period or the artist's biography. Address a general academic
LENGTH	audience in a paper about four pages long.

STRATEGY Analyze your assignment.

- What does the assignment call the task? Does that name seem to be common in the field, or is it your instructor's own creation?
- How long and how formal should your paper be?
- What topic, answer to a specific question, approach, or type of information is required? What can *you* decide?
- What key words and verbs signal what you need to do?
- Does any course guide, sample reading, or grading scale supply clues about structure, style, voice, content, or criteria for the task?
- How has your instructor explained the nature, purpose, or complexity of the task? (Take notes during any discussion.)

8b Writing goals and plans

Given your assignment's purpose, plan your approach and activities.

- Do you need to inform readers by presenting knowledge objectively? If so, present balanced facts and details. Use chunks, patterns, or a sequence to help readers understand.
- Do you need to make the case for your interpretation or evaluation? If so, present your arguments, claims, and values. Use reasons and evidence to support them and counter others.

Also consider what thinking processes are expected. The art history assignment asks you to *interpret* a work of art—not to describe it or the artist's life. Verbs like *argue, document,* and *summarize* also point to an activity that would shape a paper.

8c Common types of general academic writing

If you are unfamiliar with the type of writing assigned, analyze the assignment (see 8a), look for examples, and ask your teacher about the characteristics, structure, and style expected. Here are seven common types.

Summary. A summary presents concisely, in your own words, the main content of a longer text, a source, or original research (see 14a.)

- Begin with a one- to two-sentence overview of the work.
- Provide enough detail to convey the main ideas concisely.
- Present the work objectively without evaluation (unless assigned).

TYPES OF ACADEMIC WRITING		
TYPE	**CHARACTERISTIC ACTIVITIES**	**COMMON FORMS**
DRAWING ON SOURCES	Summarizing, paraphrasing, synthesizing, analyzing, comparing, compiling, evaluating	Summaries, abstracts, syntheses, book reviews and reports, annotated bibliographies, research papers, poster sessions, analyses of issues
REFLECTING	Responding, reacting, speculating, exploring, inquiring	Reading journals, logs (data and insights), personal essays, reaction papers, autobiographies, reflexive writing (self-observing)
INTERPRETING	Analyzing, defining key ideas, identifying causes and effects, describing patterns, applying a theory, drawing a conclusion, taking a stand on an issue	Interpretations of a text or work of art, analyses of phenomena (historical, social, or cultural), "thesis" papers taking a stand on scholarly issues, documented arguments
OBSERVING/ EXPERIMENTING	Making observations, designing surveys and experiments; collecting, synthesizing, and analyzing data; recognizing patterns	Scientific reports and articles, logs of observations and experiments, lab reports, field research reports, project evaluations
TESTING	Explaining, supporting, defining, presenting information and ideas, offering conclusions	Essay tests, take-home exams, sentence- or paragraph-length answers, responses to readings

Annotated bibliography. As in a regular bibliography (see 11e–f), each entry identifies a source. Then the annotation describes or summarizes its aim, purpose, or contents in a sentence or two.

- Follow the expected documentation style (see Part 3).
- Represent the work briefly but accurately.
- Arrange entries alphabetically, sometimes grouped by date or topic.

> Glazer, Nathan. "Where Is Multiculturalism Leading Us?" <u>Phi Delta Kappan</u>
>
> 75 (1993): 319-24. This article describes the Center for the Study of
>
> Books in Spanish for Children and Adolescents. Glazer argues that
>
> this model program promotes the positive aspects of bilingualism.

Literature review. A literature review provides an overview or a synthesis of existing research on a topic, often to justify your own research as part of a longer paper or a separate assignment.

- Specify the topic, issue, or problem that is the focus.
- Identify and summarize fairly other researchers' work (see 14a).
- Organize chronologically or thematically.

Essay exam. An answer to an essay exam responds concisely to all parts of one or more questions during the allotted time.

- Follow directions, plan quickly, and answer the question.
- Organize simply but logically with a thesis and evidence (see 2b, 3b).
- Refer to information and synthesize to support a point (see 14c).

Short documented paper. This short version of the research paper draws on a few sources and argues, interprets, or presents information.

- Summarize and synthesize others' views and positions (see 14a, 14c).
- Organize clearly to support a thesis and make reading easy (see 3b–c).
- Follow the expected documentation style (see Part 3).

Position paper. A position paper persuasively supports an assertion or a stand on an issue or a controversy.

- Avoid topics based on personal preferences, indisputable facts, and religious beliefs or other convictions (see 7a–b).
- Introduce the issue, and then state a thesis or position (see 7b).
- Use factual knowledge, statistics, logical reasoning, or selected anecdotes to support your thesis and assertions (see 7c).
- Discuss other points of view, and cite sources (see Part 3).

Review. A review is a critical appraisal of an event, an object, or a phenomenon to help people make decisions or compare judgments. A **critique** justifies a more subjective, often fresh, critical reaction.

- Describe and analyze to provide background for the reader.
- Evaluate using criteria and details to support your opinion.

9 | Writing in the Disciplines

Advanced courses, often with higher course numbers for majors, expect discipline-based writing using forms, styles, and structures shaped by the community of people who work in a field.

9a Writing in the arts and humanities

The humanities include history, languages, philosophy, literature, classics, art history, music, performing arts, cultural studies, and related areas. Writing in these fields develops theories to understand our lives and cultures, looks for patterns of meaning in the past and anticipates the future, and evaluates written and visual texts of all kinds. It **analyzes** to understand the elements and techniques of a work and **interprets** to understand the relationship of the elements and the overall meaning of the work or its context and culture.

| STRATEGY | Analyze first, and then interpret. |

- Break your subject into components and study how they relate to each other, work together, fit within a larger system, or divide into a smaller system.
- Look for patterns, connections, and relationships within the whole. Then look for the meaning that the patterns suggest.

Writers often call attention in literature to characters, plot, symbolism, and figurative language; in art to color, shadow, line, and perspective; in film to camera technique, lighting, and juxtaposition of scene. In addition, such works may convey meaning through a representation of human activity: the events of a story, a confrontation between characters, a monologue or dialogue, a scene or a setting. Interpretation can also vary with the writer's perspective: from a psychological viewpoint, you might examine a character's struggle with feelings of childhood abandonment; from a feminist perspective, you might examine the portrayal of women in a novel.

9b Common types of writing in the arts and humanities

Besides appraising creative work in reviews or critiques (see 8c), writing in the humanities also analyzes and interprets imaginative literature (fiction, poetry, drama, film).

Original interpretation. An original interpretation presents and supports your own analysis of a work.

- Make a clear point about meaning or technique.
- Use evidence from the work to support your assertions.
- Organize so a reader can easily follow the parts of your essay.

Researched interpretation. This type of analysis includes and evaluates the interpretations or commentary of others.

- Make a clear point about meaning or technique, drawing on the interpretations of others.
- Integrate and document all source material (see Part 3).

Literary text analysis. A literary text analysis examines elements of the meaning or technique of a work such as a short story, poem, or play.

- State a thesis that spells out your conclusions about the work.
- Support your analysis with specific examples of the characters, settings, events, and language of the text.
- Explain how you interpret or relate those details and examples so that a reader can see the connections that you see.

Visual text analysis. A visual text analysis examines elements of the meaning or technique of still or moving visuals (ads, photos, graphics, films).

- State a thesis that spells out your conclusions about the work.
- Support your analysis with specific elements you can observe such as color, style, form, arrangement, and realism.
- Explain how you interpret or relate those details and examples so that a reader can see the same connections you see.

9c Writing in the social and natural sciences

The social sciences are as varied as psychology, sociology, political science, economics, education, and business. Such fields examine individual and group characteristics, behaviors, and relationships. The natural sciences include scientific and medical fields: biology, physics, and chemistry as well as pharmacy, anatomy, oceanography, and meteorology. These fields investigate the rocks, oceans, stars, chemicals, and atoms of the natural world as well as its inhabitants, from tiny organisms to complex humans.

Writing in the social and natural sciences advances knowledge through measurable, objective data gathered from field observations, surveys, interviews, microscopic study, clinical notes, medical trials, and experiments in labs or facilities such as wind tunnels. Despite its variety, scientific writing often follows a prescribed format or structure.

Introduction. Explain your investigation, review prior research, and state your research questions or the hypothesis that you will test.

Methods. Describe your research design, methodology, and any procedures, materials, or measuring tools. Justify them if necessary. Mention problems or notable events during your study. Include survey or interview questions in the report or an appendix.

Results. Present your results or findings, the detailed data from the study. Add tables or graphs that make the data easy to grasp.

Discussion. Explain what your results mean and to what extent you have answered your questions or supported your hypothesis.

Conclusion. Highlight your broad results and directions for further research.

STRATEGY **Study existing texts of the same type.**

- Does the text follow a standard scientific organization?
- How does the text use subheadings or other organizing elements?
- What are the features of its language, tone, and style?
- How is the text laid out? How does it use tables and figures?
- How does it integrate and acknowledge other studies?

9d Common types of writing in the social and natural sciences

Scientific writing inquires and reports, often using conventional formats.

Abstract. An abstract is a special form of summary (see 8c, 14a) that often precedes and sums up a report or study. It previews a text to help readers assess its usefulness.

- Open with an overview expressed in a sentence or two.
- Sum up concisely all the major sections of the paper.
- Supply the reader with an accurate, objective preview.

Informative report. The informative report gathers research-based details, ideas, and conclusions relevant to a problem, solution, or policy.

- Draw on recent, reliable research studies for information.
- Provide clear explanations accessible to readers.
- Organize to emphasize important or useful aspects.
- Add visuals such as tables, graphs, and figures for clarity.

Lab report. A lab report presents procedures and outcomes of an experiment.

- Follow the exact style and format required.
- Describe accurately what happened during the experiment.
- Use specific terms and clear language. Avoid unneeded commentary.

Research report. A research report explains a tightly focused study that aims to answer a particular question.

- Follow the standard scientific format, but add narrative or descriptive evidence for a case study or a long-term observation.
- Include a review of the recent literature or a brief history for background in your introduction.

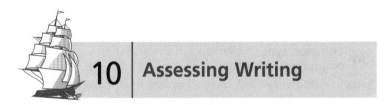

10 | Assessing Writing

Improve your writing by learning to assess it.

10a Assessing your own writing

How should you revise? What should you change? When you evaluate your own writing, try to stand "outside" the text, reading it as if you were another reader, not the writer. Make sure your writing is clear for someone who may not share your knowledge and perspective.

> **STRATEGY** Create a logical, workable plan for revision.

- Try *saying*—out loud—what you want to say. Reread your draft, and try to make it say what you mean.
- Make a numbered list of your feelings toward your subject, including values and beliefs you want readers to share. Assess your draft by numbering the places where you express those feelings.
- Place an asterisk in your draft anywhere you know you took a shortcut or wrote too quickly. Expand or refine that section.
- Set priorities for global changes. What do you need to add, delete, or re-organize? Do you need to change your tone or style?
- Edit to improve coherence, style, word choice, and the like.

10b Assessing someone else's writing

As responder, strike a helpful tone. Compliment the positives, but supply honest, useful feedback as a reader. Make a few meaningful comments; don't litter the draft with corrections. As a writer, accept criticism gratefully, but make your own final decisions.

> **STRATEGY** Be a reader, not a critic.

- Share images of your own experience: "I felt like you were beating me over the head here." Let the writer revise accordingly.
- Add checks in the margins where the writing works well and asterisks where it feels choppy, unorganized, or confusing.
- Place exclamation marks where information interests you and downward arrows where you lose focus or become bored.
- List the three most important improvements you'd recommend, such as revising an overly clinical tone or clarifying the structure.
- Mark just one case of a small problem, such as a missing apostrophe, and explain what it does to you as a reader. Let the writer find the other instances.

10c Understanding how others assess your writing

Your peers can be good "trial" readers for a paper or portfolio, but you also need to develop an internal monitor for what readers in your community like or dislike. You want to make a good impression, drawing readers into your ideas without distracting page designs, disorganized writing, or irritating errors. You also want to give them clues about where they are going by using topic sentences, transitions, and possibly headings.

> **STRATEGY** **Meet readers' expectations.**
>
> - List three important expectations your readers will have of the genre or type of writing you're creating. Consider these criteria for assessment.
> - Work through your draft once for each expectation, judging how well you achieve it. Revise, as needed, for each feature.

10d Assessing your portfolio

A portfolio is a collection of your writing, assembled for class, work, or a job interview. When a portfolio is assigned, follow carefully the directions about what to include. You'll often need to select writing that represents you at your best, following several criteria, or standards, for judging such as these.

- Choose samples that show—or after revision could show—your strengths as a writer. Decide what writing you want to present: your clearest? most improved? most convincing? best developed?
- Choose samples that show your range. Decide which selections show flexibility—perhaps your clarity, humor, and style.
- Choose informative and argumentative samples that show variety in purpose, topic, arrangement, or use of sources.

Introduce your portfolio with a brief essay that explains your selections and highlights the quality of your writing, considering topics like these.

Notable features	Your revision choices
Contrasts among pieces	Your growth as a writer
Criteria for selection	Your attention to readers

Voices
from the Community

"Research is formalized curiosity. It is poking and prying with a purpose."

—Zora Neale Hurston, *Dust Tracks on a Road*

11 | Planning and Conducting Research

Effective research writers blend their own insights with material from print, electronic, or field sources. They develop and support their ideas or provide accurate—and accessible—information. Their choices depend on both the topic and their audience or community. The same researcher might write a psychology paper on stress, a proposal for company-sponsored child care, and a report on options for a city sports league. But each task would require different research questions, strategies, sources, and ways of turning inquiry into writing.

Writers, readers, and researchers interested in a subject form a **research community,** a web of people and texts that (1) share a perspective and focus—a **research topic,** (2) agree on **research questions** worth asking, and (3) use shared terms, **keywords** that form a **research thread** linking topics and resources.

11a Recognizing research topics

Good research topics grow from the shared interests of a community of writers and readers, from recent events, or from current developments in knowledge. An assignment may launch your research project by specifying topics, deadlines, formats, and kinds of sources required by an instructor, supervisor, or organization.

> **STRATEGY** Focus your inquiry using questions.
> - What problem, issue, question, or event piques my curiosity?
> - What new, contradictory, or intriguing ideas turn up in reading?
> - What ideas do Web sites, class discussion, or meetings suggest?
> - What would my readers like to know?

AUDIENCE EXPECTATIONS FOR RESEARCH WRITING			
	ACADEMIC	**PUBLIC**	**WORK**
GOAL	Explain, interpret, analyze, synthesize	Support policy or action	Document problems, propose, improve
READER EXPECTATIONS	Detailed evidence, varied sources	Accessible, fair persuasion	Clear, precise, direct information
TYPICAL QUESTIONS	What does it mean? Why does it happen?	How can we improve a policy or situation?	What is the problem? How can we solve it?
TYPICAL FORMS	Paper to interpret, inform, or argue	Speech, pamphlet, letter, fact sheet	Proposal, feasibility study, report
SAMPLE RESEARCH QUESTION ON COSMETICS	What gender roles do ads reinforce?	Are animal tests of cosmetics necessary?	How can we develop local packaging?

11b Identifying keywords

Libraries, search engines, and databases use keywords to locate information. Recurring words (*alcohol*), names (*Mary Cassatt*), and phrases (*early childhood, string theory*) help you identify, define, and limit a topic.

STRATEGY **Identify and use keywords in research and writing.**

- Start by listing keywords that might refer to your topic, including synonyms (*maturation* for *growth*).
- Add keywords from sources; drop any that appear rarely. Use your list to search library catalogs, databases, and the Web.
- If your keywords produce too many possible sources, try more precise terms used by writers on your topic.
- Integrate keywords into your research questions and thesis.

11c Developing research questions

Create research questions to guide your inquiry, filter information, and form a basis for your **thesis**, the main idea that you explore, support, or illustrate.

Academic. What do experts ask or say about my topic? Do I agree or disagree? What can I add? What ambiguities remain?

Public. What policy or program do I propose? Whom does it benefit? Why? What might its effects be?

Work. What is the problem or situation? What do I propose? Why will it work, work better, or cost less?

Summer Arrigo-Nelson and Jennifer Figliozzi developed these research questions on student drinking for a report on a campus problem.

- Will students with permission to drink at home have different drinking behaviors at college than those without such permission?
- Do students feel that a correlation exists between drinking behaviors at home and at college?

STRATEGY State your research questions early in your inquiry.

- Aim for two or three direct questions, and embed your keywords.
- Pose real questions that call for research, not ones with easy answers or an obvious consensus.
- Formulate questions that will matter to your audience.

11d Developing critical search strategies

For most topics, print and electronic resources will provide abundant information. What you need is a **critical search strategy** to help identify the most appropriate resources for your questions and thesis (see 2b, 3b).

STRATEGY **Design a critical search strategy.**

- **List kinds of resources.** Name categories you will explore: books, scholarly journals, Web sites, databases, newspapers, interviews, surveys.
- **Identify search tools.** Consult print indexes and search engines.
  - Magazine and newspaper articles—*InfoTrac, New York Times Index*
  - Academic articles in scholarly journals—*Social Sciences Index, MLA International Bibliography, Education Index*
  - Web sites, discussion lists, and indexed databases—*Google Scholar, Highbeam Research, AltaVista, CataList, Dogpile, PAIS*
  - Academic and professional databases with built-in search engines—*EBSCOhost, LexisNexis, OCLC FirstSearch*
- **Use keywords and research questions.** List keywords (see 11b) for finding potential resources in indexes, in databases, and on the Web.
- **Revise.** Update your research questions, search strategy, and keywords as your research evolves.

11e Maintaining a working bibliography

Build a **working bibliography** of possible sources that address your research questions. Consult indexes, catalogs, search engines, or databases (see 12a–e, 13a) for relevant, credible possibilities.

Include
- Recent and varied sources, from broad surveys to focused studies
- Items whose titles sound relevant to your research questions
- Selections from bibliographies with *annotations* or from search engines with *abstracts* that summarize content and perspective
- Critical sources that review or evaluate recent developments or other research
- More sources than needed, to allow for any not available or not useful

11f Keeping track of sources and notes

Record bibliographic information for your sources, take notes (14a–b), and record source evaluations (15a–c) using one of three methods.

Note cards. Cards are easy to group or to add. Write each bibliography entry on a 3" × 5" card and each reading note on a 4" × 6" card.

Research notebook. In a notebook you can add marginal notes, attach colored dots or flags, or duplicate pages to cut up as you organize.

Electronic notes. Note-taking or word-processing programs easily transfer to a reference list or draft paper. Some programs will format entries using the documentation style you select.

Link your notes to keywords or research questions and to page numbers in your sources. Record the following information about sources.

BOOKS	**ARTICLES**	**ELECTRONIC SOURCES**
Author(s), editor(s), translator(s)	Author(s)	Name of source
Title: Subtitle	Title: Subtitle	Author or sponsoring group
City: publisher, date	Periodical name	Address/URL/access route/vendor
Call number and library location	Volume (& issue) number(s)	Name of database
	Date	Date of publication or last revision
	Page number(s)	Date of access
	Library location	

11g Assembling your research materials

Manage the information you locate with these strategies.

- Gather your notes, copies, printouts, files, and other material.
- Sort your resources, and track down missing material.
- Use your research questions as guides to main points and subtopics. Use keywords, color coding, or stacks of material to sort by category.
- Drop a category containing little information, or do more research. Consider splitting an abundant category into subtopics.
- Consult a librarian, instructor, or specialist in the field if you need more information.

12 | Finding Library and Database Resources

Before the electronic revolution, researchers struggled to gain access to relatively scarce sources, many unavailable locally. Now increasing and available electronic resources require researchers to sift through abundant options for appropriate, reliable, and insightful sources.

Libraries and research databases offer one set of challenges; the Web and the Internet offer another (see 13a–b). However, both supply two major types of sources. **Primary sources** provide information in original (or close-to-original) form: historical and literary texts, letters, videos, survey results, and other data. **Secondary sources** explain, analyze, or interpret primary sources, telling you what others have said and what issues are debated by scholars and other writers.

12a Finding library resources

Libraries give you access to resources that serve academic, public, and work interests. Start with **ready references:** general encyclopedias, atlases, dictionaries, and statistical abstracts. Then turn to **specialized encyclopedias** and **dictionaries,** as varied as *Current Biography* and the *Encyclopedia of Pop, Rock, and Soul*. Check useful **bibliographies,** listings of resources such as the *MLA International Bibliography* on literature and language or the *International Bibliography of the Social Sciences*.

STRATEGY Talk to information specialists.

Reference librarians can help you refine a search strategy, improve keyword searches, and locate materials on campus or on loan.

12b Locating books

Start with the author's name, a title, or keywords. Use them to search the library home page or online catalog. When a **brief display** lists several items, click on one to call up its **full display.** Expand a search to related topics, authors, or works, or follow related links. Print or record your results, with call numbers and locations.

12c Locating periodicals and other documents

Periodicals appear regularly with articles by many authors. **Online periodicals** may place past articles in electronic archives; other **Web sites** act like periodicals, adding material as the site is updated. **Periodical indexes** list articles and may supply brief summaries (or abstracts).

Your library offers access to **general indexes:** *InfoTrac, OCLC/World Catalog, PAIS (Public Affairs, Information Services), NewsBank.* Academic libraries also supply **specialized indexes:** *BIZZ (Business Index), Government Documents Catalog Service (GDCS/GPO Index), Current Index to Journals in Education (CIJE), Social Sciences Index, Biological and Agricultural Index.*

Government documents include reports, pamphlets, and regulations issued by Congress, federal agencies, and state or local governments. See the *Monthly Catalog of U.S. Government Publications, Library of Congress* <http://www.loc.gov>, *Thomas Legislative Information* site <http://thomas.loc.gov>, *FedStats* <http://www.fedstats.gov>, and *GPO Access* <http://www.gpoaccess.gov>.

Special collections house many documents, including those on local history. **Audiovisual collections** contain tapes, films, and recordings. **Microform collections** contain copies of periodicals and documents.

12d Finding research databases

Electronic databases contain all kinds of information, especially texts of scholarly and general-interest periodical articles. University and public libraries

PRINT PERIODICALS			
	MAGAZINES	**JOURNALS**	**NEWSPAPERS**
READERS?	General public	Academics, professionals	General public
WRITERS?	Staff, journalists	Scholars, experts	Staff, journalists
HOW OFTEN?	Monthly, weekly	Quarterly, monthly	Daily, weekly
APPEARANCE?	Color, photos, glossy paper, sidebars	Dense text, data, plain paper, little color	Columns, headlines, photos, some color

have greatly increased their specialized **online databases.** You can access them at library terminals, a library's Web site, or the Web site of a database company such as Highbeam or LexisNexis. You can generally search a database by author, title, and keyword or by categories appropriate for the collection. Most databases are updated frequently. Consult library handouts or the information screen of a database to learn what resources it provides and what range of dates it covers.

12e Locating database articles and documents

Databases vary according to the information and texts they provide.

- **Full-text databases** list articles and other documents and briefly summarize each item. In addition, they provide entire texts of most items indexed. Examples: *Academic Search Premier, Academic Universe, ArticleFirst, InfoTrac OneFile, Health Reference Center Academic.*
- **Databases containing abstracts** provide brief summaries of documents and sometimes full texts. Some link to a library's online periodical subscriptions. Examples: *PsycINFO, Sociological Abstracts, Biological Abstracts, MEDLINE, MLA Bibliography, Historical Abstracts, ERIC.*

- **Indexing or bibliographic databases** provide information for articles and documents in a specialized field. Examples: *BioONE, GEOBASE*.
- **Resource databases** either provide access to information, images, and documents arranged as an electronic reference work or offer tools for researchers. Examples: *WorldCat* (library and Internet resources worldwide); *Web of Science* (indexes identifying sources cited by researchers); *RefWorks* (help with documentation styles in a range of fields).

13 | Finding Web Resources

The abundance of Web (and Internet) resources means that appropriate sources for your research are probably available—if you can locate them among the millions of documents online.

13a Finding Web and Internet resources

You can access Web documents (**pages**) or collections of pages (**sites**) using a **browser,** such as *Internet Explorer, Firefox,* or *Safari*. Enter the Web page's address (a **URL,** or Uniform Resource Locator), or follow links in an online text. The **Internet** links researchers through email, discussion groups, and Web sites. Materials range from well-researched reports to hasty messages. See 15e for help evaluating these sources.

Search engines. General **search engines** gather data about Web sites and discussion groups. They typically search by keywords or phrases you identify. However, because each one employs its own principle of selection, turn to more than one to identify relevant resources.

```
 ┌──────────────────────────────────────────────────────┐
 │  GENERAL SEARCH ENGINES                               │
 │  Google           <http://www.google.com>            │
 │  AltaVista        <http://altavista.com>             │
 │  Yahoo!           <http://www.yahoo.com>             │
 │  AllTheWeb        <http://alltheweb.com/>            │
 │  Gigablast        <http://gigablast.com>            │
 │  Lycos            <http://www.lycos.com>             │
 │  Ask              <http://www.ask.com/>             │
 └──────────────────────────────────────────────────────┘
```

GENERAL SEARCH ENGINES	
Google	<http://www.google.com>
AltaVista	<http://altavista.com>
Yahoo!	<http://www.yahoo.com>
AllTheWeb	<http://alltheweb.com/>
Gigablast	<http://gigablast.com>
Lycos	<http://www.lycos.com>
Ask	<http://www.ask.com/>

Metasearch sites enable you to conduct your search using several search engines simultaneously—and then to compare the results.

METASEARCH SITES	
Dogpile	<http://dogpile.com>
Ixquick	<http://www.ixquick.com>
Metacrawler	<http://metacrawler.com>

Electronic messages and postings. Electronic mail (**email**) allows you to contact people who can answer questions or provide information. Search engines have directory services that can locate email addresses of individuals, and many Web pages let you email the author or sponsor.

Newsgroups and **Web discussion forums** are public sites. Anyone can post messages and read other posts. In contrast, you subscribe to **electronic mailing lists** and then check your email for messages. All these sources are conversational and may or may not supply reliable information.

13b Searching efficiently

Choose your search terms carefully. Be ready to revise them.

- Use your research questions and keywords to select search terms.
- Search engines find the exact words you specify. Type—and spell—carefully. Try various word forms and related terms.
- If a database contains items with keywords matching your search terms, the items will appear as your search results.
- Repeat a successful search, looking for other useful keywords and combinations. Use your most effective clusters to search additional databases.

A string of keywords or specific terms is called a **query.** Use your query to narrow a search by grouping terms, specifying those you want to combine, rule out, or treat as alternatives.

STRATEGY **Use advanced search strategies.**

If your search produces too many or too few items, try the advanced search strategies for the search engine or index. Many use these markers.

OR (expands): Search for either term
  X OR Y → documents referring to either X or Y
AND (restricts): Search for both terms
  X AND Y → documents referring to both X and Y
NOT (excludes): Search for X unless X includes Y
  X NOT Y → documents referring to X unless they refer to Y

Search engines may automatically combine terms when you enter more than one word (*college drinking policy*) or ask you to use signs (*college + alcohol*) or words (*early childhood education NOT Head Start*).

13c Locating appropriate Web resources

To make effective use of Web resources, you should be able to recognize some important kinds of Web sites and understand their uses.

- **Individual Web sites** are maintained by, but are not necessarily *about,* individuals. **Home pages** may share lives, interests, or research; **blogs** may record thoughts and actions in newsworthy settings.

- **Advocacy Web sites** promote an organization's beliefs and policies. Although they favor the organization's position, many explain positions, answer critics, and provide detailed evidence and documentation.
- **Informational Web sites** focus on a subject such as sleep research, horror movies, or poetry from the 1950s Beat Generation. Their reliability varies, but the best are clearly organized, informative, and trustworthy.
- **Research-oriented Web sites,** sponsored by universities, research institutes, or professional organizations, typically contain (1) full texts of research reports, (2) summaries, (3) downloadable data in tables and graphs, (4) reviews of current research, (5) texts of unpublished papers and presentations, and (6) bibliographies of books, articles, or links.

14 | Reading and Synthesizing Sources

Research writing that presents ideas and information taken directly from sources, especially when long quotations are strung together, is ineffective. It neither meets the reader's expectations nor offers the writer's insights. Instead, your audience expects you to read and interpret sources and then draw on them for your own purposes.

14a Summarizing

Summarize a source to compress its ideas in forms useful for writing.

STRATEGY Summarize a source.

- **Read** carefully, underlining, highlighting, or noting key ideas, supporting evidence, and other information.

- **Scan** (reread quickly) to decide which ideas and information are most important. Identify the major purpose and sections of the selection.
- **Sum up** the key ideas of *each section* in *one sentence*.
- **Capture the main point** of the *entire passage* in *one sentence*.
- **Combine** your section summaries with your overall summary.
- **Revise** for clarity. Check against the source for accuracy.
- **Document** your source using a standard style (see Part 3).

Summer Arrigo-Nelson and Jennifer Figliozzi used summary sentences to introduce a research question, noting sources in APA style (see 18a–c).

First, research has shown that adolescents who have close relationships with parents use alcohol less often than do those with conflictual relationships (Sieving, 1996). For example, a survey of students in grades 7 to 12 reported that about 35% were under parental supervision while drinking (Department of Education, 1993).

14b Paraphrasing

Paraphrase the content of a source in your own words with your own focus to help you integrate its ideas with your own.

STRATEGY Paraphrase a source.
- **Read** carefully to understand both the wording and the content.
- **Write** a draft using your own words in place of the original. You may retain names, proper nouns, and the like from the original.
- **Revise** for smooth reading and clarity.
- **Document** your source clearly using a standard style (see Part 3).

Jennifer Figliozzi read this passage in a *Chronicle of Higher Education* article on current alcohol abuse programs at various schools:

The university also now notifies parents when their sons or daughters violate the alcohol policy, or any other aspect of the student code of conduct. "We were hoping that the support of parents would help change students' behavior, and we believe it has," says Timothy H. Brooks, an assistant vice-president and the dean of students.

To integrate this information smoothly, Jennifer combined a paraphrase with a brief quotation and cited it using APA style (see 18a–c).

Officials at the University of Delaware thought that letting parents know when students violate regulations on alcohol use would alter students' drinking habits, and one administrator now says, "we believe it has" (Reisberg, 1998, p. A42).

14c Synthesizing

When you synthesize several sources, you explore connections among their conclusions, evidence, and perspectives. Your synthesis may relate ideas, investigate differences, or build links to your research question.

> **STRATEGY**   **Synthesize sources to highlight their relationships.**
>
> - **Gather and read** your sources.
> - **Focus** on the purpose and role of your synthesis, and draft a sentence summing up your conclusion about the relationship of the sources.
> - **Arrange** your sources in a logical order of presentation.
> - **Write** a draft synthesis, presenting summaries of sources, offering your conclusion about the relationships, and acknowledging contradictions.
> - **Revise** for smooth reading and clear identification of sources.
> - **Document** your sources clearly using a standard style (see Part 3).

In his paper on conspiracy theories, Sam Roles synthesized his sources to provide background on why conspiracy theories are hard to refute. He followed MLA style (see 17a–c).

Conspiracy theories arise, according to scholars, for a number of reasons:

political fragmentation and suspicion of difference (Pipes), something

to occupy the imagination of a bored subculture (Fenster), and fear of more powerful groups (Johnson). For example, in the 1950s and 1960s,

communism provided a . . .

14d Questioning

When you question your sources, you can go beyond them to develop ideas and insights of your own. Consider gathering questions about the ideas and information in a source—questions worth sharing with readers—into a problem paragraph.

STRATEGY   Create a problem paragraph.

Challenge a source in a paragraph on problems or limitations.
Lily Germaine prepared this note card on bodybuilding.

Tucker, pp. 389-91   Weight training & self-concept

Tucker uses "although" at least four times when summarizing
other studies. He's nice on the surface but sets his readers up
to find fault with other studies that lack objective
methodology. But he thinks he can be completely objective about
such a slippery thing as "self-concept." I really question this.

Lily's problem paragraph incorporated her insights.

   Does bodybuilding affect self-concept? Before we can answer this question, we need to ask if we can accurately measure such a slippery thing as "self-concept." Some researchers, like Tucker, believe that self-concept can be accurately gauged by mathematical measurements and rigid definitions of terms. For several reasons, however, this assumption is questionable.

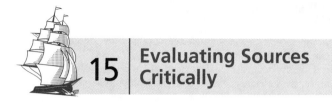

15 | Evaluating Sources Critically

Choosing from the flood of potential sources calls for critical evaluation.

15a Evaluating appropriateness

Just because a potential source addresses your topic doesn't mean it suits your work. It may cover information you already have or issues outside your topic. As you read its title and abstract or skim it, keep your research questions in mind (see 11c).

> **STRATEGY** Interpret and assess to show appropriateness.
>
> - State the source's conclusions accurately.
> - Interpret the source, and justify its role in your discussion.
> - Assess its value, noting reasonable judgments or solid examples.

15b Evaluating accuracy and reliability

When you turn to a source for information you don't have, you are unlikely to be an expert judge of its accuracy or reliability. Instead, you need to rely on the judgment of experts or on evidence within the source. Most printed books and periodicals (and their electronic versions) reflect the expert attention of reviewers, editors, and publishers. On the Web, however, anyone can present outdated or bogus information as reliable, accurate, or research-based.

> **STRATEGY** Evaluate the accuracy and reliability of a source.
>
> - Who or what is it? What can you tell about its trustworthiness?
> - What are the author's or sponsor's credentials or reputation?

- What processes has it gone through before publication? Was it evaluated by reviewers or an editorial board?
- Do others discuss or cite it? Do they view it as authoritative?
- Does it meet the standards of your research community?
- Is it grounded on current research or credible authority?
- Does it cite sources or clearly attribute ideas? Does a site link to credible sites that support its discussion?
- Does a site name its author or sponsor? Does the author of a blog, email message, or discussion posting seem to have expertise?
- Is the information credible? Is it presented logically with evidence? Does it recognize alternatives and complexities?

15c Evaluating point of view or bias

Having a point of view is not wrong, but the thesis in an academic, public, or work report should make the writer's perspective clear.

- What opinion or thesis does the writer endorse? Does the writer acknowledge other points of view and treat them fairly?
- Does the source intend to inform, advocate, or do something else? Does it separate fact from opinion or present opinion as fact?
- How accurate is the source? Are its ideas consistent with those in other sources? Are they insightful or misleading?
- How does the writer support statements? Do claims exceed facts?
- Does the source cite experts with political or financial interests? Does it try to hide its viewpoint?

15d Evaluating search engine results

Search engines usually rank sites based on their match with a query, but the first sites they list may not be the best for your needs. *Google* combines number of visitors with matches to a query. *Digg* asks users to vote and comment on a site's value. Don't let "popularity" replace critical evaluation; sites lower in the list may add fresh details.

A WORD ABOUT *WIKIPEDIA*

Wikipedia, an online encyclopedia, covers many topics, including definitions of terms and concepts. Unlike print encyclopedias created by experts, *Wikipedia* is constantly updated by its users, some of whom are experts, some not. Like a print encyclopedia, it can be a good place to start learning about a topic, but as a source it has two serious limitations.

1. *Wikipedia* presents what is generally known, not original research. If you use it as a source, you'll repeat, not add to, what readers know.
2. *Wikipedia* users edit entries for accuracy and objectivity. Some are experts, but many are students, so the quality can be uneven.

15e Evaluating Web sources critically

To evaluate Web sources, ask the questions developed by Paula Mathieu and Ken McAllister for the CRITT (Critical Resources in Teaching with Technology) project at the University of Illinois at Chicago.

- **Who benefits? What difference does that make?** These questions can alert you to the perspective of the source and its effect on accuracy or trustworthiness. The site at <http://www.gotmilk.com/>, for example, seems dedicated to the reader's health (see Figure 15.1). But because this site promotes drinking milk and eating milk products, dairy farmers and milk processors will also benefit from sales.
- **Who's talking? What difference does that make?** These questions help you assess reliability and the likelihood of balance or bias. The "speaker" for the site's positive facts about milk is not clearly identified, but the site's privacy policy for its store and its press releases mention the California Milk Processor Board, one of many milk-industry associations. What might be the point of view of these groups? Will all the "facts" appear, especially any that question milk's goodness?

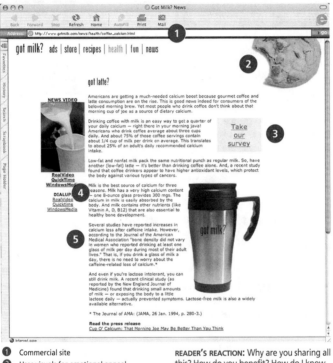

1. Commercial site
2. Uses visuals for emotional appeal
3. Links milk to healthier coffee
4. Explains nutritional benefits of milk
5. Cites studies to advocate drinking milk

READER'S REACTION: Why are you sharing all this? How do you benefit? How do I know this is accurate, complete information?

FIGURE 15.1 "Got Latte?" Web page

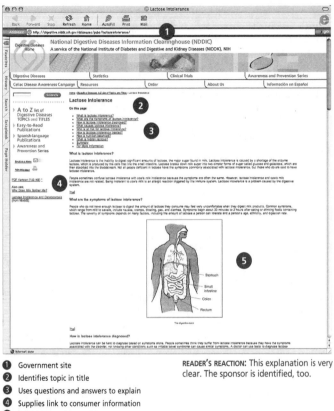

① Government site

② Identifies topic in title

③ Uses questions and answers to explain

④ Supplies link to consumer information

⑤ Adds informative graphics

READER'S REACTION: This explanation is very clear. The sponsor is identified, too.

FIGURE 15.2   "Lactose Intolerance" Web page

In contrast, the Web page at <http://digestive.niddk.nih.gov/ddiseases/pubs/lactoseintolerance/> (see Figure 15.2) clearly and impartially answers questions about lactose intolerance, a widespread inability to digest milk sugar. The "speaker" is an authoritative government agency—the National Digestive Diseases Information Clearinghouse, part of the National Institutes of Health.

- **What's missing? What difference does that make?** The *Got Milk* site is a commercial venture promoting cow's milk. Naturally it ignores soy, goat, and other milk (and nonmilk) options. On the other hand, "Lactose Intolerance" does not promote or attack dairy products; instead, its reliable advice ignores commercial and other interests. Each of these Web sites—like every other resource—has a point of view or vested interest that guides its selection and presentation of information.

15f Turning inquiry into writing

After you locate (see 12a–e) and read (see 1b and 14a–b) useful sources, you're ready to pull your research together and think strategically.

- Consider what you want your readers to learn, do, or feel.
- Place your research questions in a trial sequence. Refine them.
- State, extend, and modify your rough thesis. Break it into easy-to-read sentences or restate it to show your reasoning (see 2a–b).
- Anticipate and respond to your readers' possible reactions.
- Group materials and arrange them in sequence. Connect the chunks.
- Draft an introduction and conclusion around your research questions.
- Draft the middle so readers can follow your reasoning, see your evidence, and accept your conclusions. Don't just pack in details.
- Ask readers to respond to a draft. Revise, edit, proofread (1c), and design your document (see 6a–d). Quote accurately, cite page numbers and authors correctly, and check your documentation form (Part 3).

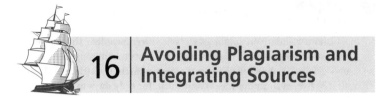

16 | Avoiding Plagiarism and Integrating Sources

By distinguishing your contributions from those of your sources, you'll get credit for your insights and hard work. You'll also avoid inadvertently taking credit for the work of others—a form of theft called **plagiarism.** Carefully integrating and citing sources adds to your credibility, substantiates your knowledge, and allows readers to draw on your research.

16a Avoiding plagiarism

As you quote, paraphrase, or summarize, you *must* cite sources.

- Enclose someone's exact words in quotation marks.
- Paraphrase and summarize in your own words.
- Cite the source of whatever you integrate.

Without quotation marks, the following paraphrase is too close to the original and would be seen as plagiarized because the writer made only minor changes in some phrases and "lifted" others verbatim.

ORIGINAL PASSAGE

Malnutrition was a widespread and increasingly severe problem throughout the least developed parts of the world in the 1970s, and would continue to be serious, occasionally reaching famine conditions, as the millennium approached. Among the cells of the human body most dependent upon a steady source of nutrients are those of the immune system, most of which live, even under ideal conditions, for only days at a time. (From Laurie Garrett, *The Coming Plague*, New York: Penguin, 1994, p. 199.)

PLAGIARIZED VERSION

In her book about emerging global diseases, Garrett points out that malnutrition can give microbes an advantage as they spread through the population. Malnutrition continues to be a **severe problem throughout the least developed parts of the world.** The human immune system contains cells that are **dependent upon a steady source of nutrients.** These cells may **live, even under ideal conditions, for only days at a time.**

APPROPRIATE PARAPHRASE

In her book about emerging global diseases, Garrett points out that malnutrition can give microbes an advantage as they spread through the population. The human body contains immune cells that help to fight off various diseases. When the body is deprived of nutrients, these immune cells will weaken (Garrett 199).

APPROPRIATE SUMMARY

Malnutrition can so weaken people's immune systems that diseases they would otherwise fight off can gain an advantage (Garrett 199).

16b Deciding what to document

In general, document words, ideas, and information from another's work. Add credibility by showing your careful research, acknowledging someone's hard work, and giving others access to your sources. Also consider your readers. General readers may expect sources when you identify subatomic particles; physicists would probably assume this is common knowledge.

You *Must* Document
- Word-for-word (direct) quotations from a source
- Paraphrases or summaries of someone else's work, whether published or presented orally or electronically
- Ideas, opinions, and interpretations that others have developed, even those based on common knowledge
- Facts or data someone has gathered or identified, unless the information is considered common knowledge
- Information that is disputed or not widely accepted
- Visuals, recordings, performances, interviews, and the like

But *Do Not* Document
- Ideas, opinions, and interpretations that are your own

- Widely known information available in common reference works or generally seen as common knowledge
- Commonly used quotations ("To be, or not to be")

16c Documenting sources for different audiences

Each community has its own expectations about using sources.

Academic. Academic readers generally expect you to show how your ideas fit into a research tradition. They look for authoritative evidence and documentation appropriate to the field. Integrate sources—quotations, findings, currency, or other matters—to meet their expectations.

Public. Public readers may appreciate source material and be content with informal citations. But when you advocate a policy or offer controversial interpretations, readers expect fair play and accurate detail.

Work. Readers at work expect brief treatment of what they know and extended treatment of what they don't (but need to). They may expect quotations, paraphrases, summaries, or visuals—all documented.

16d Integrating quotations

Select a quotation carefully, identify the source, retain its exact wording, and use it to support your points.

You can quote entire sentences:

Celebrities can also play roles in our fantasy lives: "Many people admire, but do not mimic, the audacity of the rebellious rock star" (McVey 32).

Or you can embed a quotation of a few words or lines.

Many teens were "riveted by Dylan's lyrical cynicism" (Low 124).

POSSIBLE CONTRIBUTIONS OF QUOTATIONS

- Bolster your conclusions with a recognized authority.
- Convey ideas accurately, stylishly, concisely, or persuasively.

- Provide a jumping-off point, change of pace, or vivid example.

GUIDELINES FOR ADDING QUOTATIONS

- Put the exact spoken or written words of your source in quotation marks. Introduce and connect the quotation smoothly, interpreting for readers. Mention the source in your text or a citation.
- Use a colon only after an introductory line that is a complete sentence. Use commas to set off tags such as "*X* said" that introduce or interrupt a quotation. Otherwise, use the context to determine the punctuation.
- Review related conventions: combining marks (44h), capitals (39b), and brackets and ellipses (44c–d).
- If you use a specific documentation style (see Part 3), check its advice.

Block quotations for prose. To quote a passage longer than four lines typed (MLA) or forty words (APA), begin on the line after your introduction. Indent 1" or ten spaces (MLA, see 17c) or 1/2" or five spaces (APA, see below, and 18c). Double-space but omit quotation marks (unless in the source).

If you quote from one paragraph, begin without further indentation. Otherwise, indent all paragraphs 1/4" or three spaces (MLA) or any additional paragraph 1/2" or five spaces (APA).

Perez (1998) anticipates shifts in staff training:

> The great challenge for most school districts is to earmark sufficient funds for training personnel, not for purchasing or upgrading hardware and software. The technological revolution in the average classroom will depend to a large degree on innovation in professional development. (p. 64)

Block quotations for poetry. Begin four or more lines of poetry on the line after your introduction. Indent 1" or ten spaces from the left (MLA). Double-space but omit quotation marks (unless in the verse).

Donald Hall also varies rhythm, as in "The Black-Faced Sheep."

> My grandfather spent all day searching the valley
>
> and edges of Ragged Mountain,
>
> calling "Ke-<u>day</u>!" as if he brought you salt,
>
> "Ke-<u>day</u>! Ke-<u>day</u>!" (lines 9–12)

16e Integrating sources into your text

Credit your sources, and weave their points or details into your own line of reasoning. To make your writing more sophisticated, quote selectively. Paraphrase, summarize, or synthesize instead (see 14a–c).

EMBEDDING SOURCE MATERIAL

- Select sound evidence that supports your purpose and thesis.
- Alternate striking short quotations with paraphrase and summary to avoid long, tedious quotations.
- Draw facts, details, and statistics from your sources as well as ideas and expressions. Credit these, too.
- Tell readers how to interpret or connect sources so your interpretation and reasoning shape the discussion.

Drawings, photos, tables, graphs, and charts can consolidate or explore data (see 6d). If you copy or download a visual, you'll need to cite its source, and you may need permission to use it.

STRATEGY   Integrate visuals for readers.

- Put the visual close to the relevant text without disrupting the discussion. Make sure that it explains or extends your point.
- Use clear, readable visuals in an appropriate size.
- Add labels (MLA: Table 1, Fig. 1; APA: Table 3, *Figure 1*).

16f Integrating visual and Webbed sources

In a traditional research paper, you present information from your sources as quotations, summaries, or paraphrases. Today, however, you may begin by envisioning your paper as a neat stack of pages emerging from your printer, but this is not your *only* option.

Printed document with visuals. A printed document does not have to rely on words alone. Use your word-processing program to integrate substantial information in charts, graphs, pictures, and clip art. Place the visual near the relevant written discussion so readers can see how they relate.

Presentation programs like *PowerPoint* will arrange information graphically to relate and highlight key ideas. They can also incorporate action sequences such as arrows linking statements or fades from one text or visual to another. Try using such programs within denser texts (see Figure 16.1).

FIGURE 16.1 *PowerPoint* presentation within a document

Webbed document. A Web page or a file written in HTML allows readers to move around at will within a document. Add links to online articles you summarize or paraphrase, so readers can test the accuracy of your work. Or include links to Web sites with supporting evidence or arguments. Write each section so that it can stand alone without being read in a linear way.

PART

3

Documenting Sources

Voices
from the Community

"*The* MLA Handbook for Writers of Research Papers *is designed to introduce you to the customs of a community of writers who greatly value scrupulous scholarship and the careful documentation, or recording, of research.*"

—Joseph Gibaldi, *MLA Handbook for Writers of Research Papers,* 6th ed., p. xv

"*Rules for the preparation of manuscripts should contribute to clear communication. . . . They spare readers a distracting variety of forms throughout a work and permit readers to give full attention to content.*"

—*Publication Manual of the American Psychological Association,* 5th ed., p. xxiii

GUIDE TO MLA FORMATS

MLA Formats for In-Text (Parenthetical) Citations

MLA Formats for List of Works Cited

17 | MLA Style

The MLA (Modern Language Association) documentation style is a clear system for acknowledging your sources and directing readers to them. It has two elements: a citation in the text (usually in parentheses) and a list of works cited (at the end of the text).

MLA is a simple, direct style that emphasizes scrupulous respect for ideas, information, and quotations from sources. Use it in academic settings when you write in a humanities field or your instructor asks for simple, parenthetical documentation. Consider it in public and work settings when readers favor a clear, direct style that seldom uses footnotes.

For more detailed discussion, see the *MLA Handbook for Writers of Research Papers* (6th ed., New York: MLA, 2003), the *MLA Style Manual and Guide to Scholarly Publishing* (2nd ed., New York: MLA, 1998), or updates posted on the MLA Web site <http://www.mla.org>.

17a MLA in-text (parenthetical) citations

In MLA style, you include in the text information that helps readers identify your source, described in full in the list of works cited at the end of the paper. Generally, an author's name—provided in parentheses or in your discussion—is enough to do so.

1. Author's Name in Parentheses

IN PARENTHESES   When people marry now, "there is an important sense in which
they don't know what they are doing" (Giddens 46).

2. Author's Name in Discussion

IN DISCUSSION   Giddens claims that when people marry now "they don't
know what they are doing" (46).

3. General Reference

A **general reference** refers to ideas or information throughout the source as a whole; it needs no page number.

IN PARENTHESES   Many species of animals have complex systems of

communication (Bright).

IN DISCUSSION   As Michael Bright observes, many species of animals have

complex systems of communication.

4. Specific Reference

A **specific reference** documents words, ideas, or facts from a particular place in a source, often the page from which you quote or paraphrase.

QUOTATION   Dolphins perceive clicking sounds "made up of 700 units of

sound per second" (Bright 52).

PARAPHRASE   Bright reports that dolphins recognize patterns consisting of

seven hundred clicks each second (52).

5. Specific Reference to Online Source

Add numbers for the page, paragraph (par., pars.), section (sec.), or screen (screen) if given. Otherwise, no number is needed.

WEB SITE   Offspringmag.com summarizes research on adolescents

(Boynton screen 2).

PDF FILE   The Royal College of Psychiatrists Web site says using alcohol

to get to sleep often means awakening "half-way through the

night" (4).

WEB SITE   Using alcohol to get to sleep often means awakening

"half-way through the night" (Royal).

6. Specific Reference to Other Nonprint Source

Use any available location or no number.

> The heroine's mother in the film <u>Clueless</u> died during liposuction.

7. One Author

> According to Maureen Honey, government posters during World War II often
>
> portrayed homemakers "as vital defenders of the nation's homes" (135).

8. Two or Three Authors

> The item is noted in a partial list of Francis Bacon's debts after 1602
>
> (Jardine and Stewart 275).

Follow the same pattern for three authors: (Norman, Fraser, and Jenko 209).

9. Four or More Authors

In parentheses, add *et al.* ("and others") after the first name. In your discussion, use phrases like "Chen and his colleagues." If you give all names in your Works Cited instead of *et al.*, do so in the text (see Entry 3, p. 77).

> More funding would encourage creative research (Chen et al. 1982).

10. Organization or Group Author

If an organization is named as the author, name it in the text or citation; shorten a cumbersome name (Committee of Concerned Journalists).

> The consortium gathers journalists at "a critical moment" (Committee 187).

11. No Author Given

> Czechoslovakia split into the Czech and Slovak republics (<u>Baedeker's</u> 67).

The full title is *Baedeker's Czech/Slovak Republics*.

12. More Than One Work by the Same Author

When the list of works cited contains more than one entry by an author, add a shortened title to your citation.

> Such "quaintness glorifies . . . industriousness" (Harris, Cute 46).

13. Authors with the Same Name

Add the first initial or name to distinguish the author.

> Despite improved health information systems (J. Adams 308), medical
>
> errors continue to increase (D. Adams 1).

14. Indirect Source

Use *qtd. in* ("quoted in") for a quotation or paraphrase taken from yet another source. Here, Feuch is the source of the quotation from Vitz.

> For Vitz, "art, especially great art, must engage all or almost all of the
>
> major capacities of the nervous system" (qtd. in Feuch 65).

15. Multivolume Work

You may cite a whole volume (Cao, vol. 4) or one of several used (Cao 4: 177).

> Lewis Carroll approved calling a school paper Jabberwock, a made-up
>
> word from Alice's Adventures in Wonderland (Cohen 2: 695).

16. Literary Work

After the page number in your edition, add the chapter (ch.), part (pt.), or section (sec.) number to help readers find the passage in other editions.

> In Huckleberry Finn, Mark Twain ridicules an actor who "would squeeze his
>
> hand on his forehead and stagger back and kind of moan" (178; ch. 21).

For poems, give lines: (lines 55–57), (55–57) after the first case, or (4.20–23) with a part. For plays, give act, scene, and line: (Ham. 1.2.7).

17. Sacred Text

Give book, chapter, and verse: (Mark 2.3–4). In parentheses, abbreviate names of five or more letters: (Deut. 16.21–22) for Deuteronomy.

18. Selection in Anthology

For an essay, story, poem, or other selection, cite the work's author (not the anthology's editor), but give the anthology's page numbers.

Corry shows how Internet censorship crosses party lines (112).

19. Visual in Text

Refer to a visual as a figure (fig.). Add a citation to its caption.

TEXT   Satellite photos (fig. 2) show the damage from Hurricane

                    Katrina.

FIGURE CAPTION Fig. 2. Extent of flooding on September 8, 2005 (National

                    Aeronautics and Space Administration).

20. Two or More Sources in a Citation

The different ways men and women use language can often be traced to

who has power (Tanner 83-86; Tavris 297-301).

21. Work Cited More Than Once

If you refer to a source more than once in a paragraph without another source in between, consider combining references.

Giddens views society as "a runaway world" lacking reason yet holding

"multiple possibilities" (Bryant and Jary 263, 264).

Giddens sees society as "a runaway world" (Bryant and Jary 263). Though

reason may be lacking, he finds "multiple possibilities" open (264).

22. **Informative Footnote or Endnote**

To comment on a source or add information useful to only a few readers, use a footnote or endnote. Place a superscript number (raised slightly above the line of text) at a suitable point in your paper. Provide the note itself, with the same number, as a footnote at the end of the page or as an endnote on a page titled "Notes" before the list of works cited.

[1] Before changing your eating habits, check with your doctor.

PLACEMENT AND PUNCTUATION OF PARENTHETICAL CITATIONS

Put parenthetical citations close to the quotation, information, paraphrase, or summary you are documenting.

- At the end of a sentence before the final punctuation

   Wayland Hand reports on a folk belief that going to sleep on a rug
   made of bearskin can relieve backache (183).

- After the part of a sentence to which a citation applies, at a natural pause that does not disrupt the sentence, or after the last of several quotations in a paragraph, all from one page of the same source

   The belief that "sleeping on a bear rug will cure backache" (Hand
   183) illustrates the magic of external objects acting inside
   the body.

- At the end of a long quotation set off as a block (see 16d), after the end punctuation with a space before the parentheses

   Many baseball players are superstitious, especially pitchers.

      Some pitchers refuse to walk anywhere on the day of the

      game in the belief that every little exertion subtracts

> from their playing strength. One pitcher would never put
>
> on his cap until the game started and would not wear it
>
> at all on the days he did not pitch. (Gmelch 280)

17b MLA list of works cited

Provide readers with the details for sources you cite in your text.

- Begin a list titled "Works Cited" on a new page right after your paper ends. If you include all the works you consulted, not just those you cited, call it "Works Consulted." (See p. 98 for a sample list.)
- Alphabetize by authors' last names, then by title for multiple works by the same author, and by the first main word in a title without an author.
- Do not indent the first line of each entry; indent additional lines one-half inch or five spaces.
- Double-space the entire list. Consistently leave a single space (as in print) or two spaces (if used in your text) after a period within an entry.

Books and Works Treated as Books

Provide the author's name (last name first); underlined title; city of publication, publisher in short form (*U of Chicago P* for University of Chicago Press or *McGraw* for McGraw-Hill, Inc.), and year of publication.

1. One Author

Hockney, David. <u>Secret Knowledge: Recovering the Lost Techniques of the</u>

<u>Old Masters</u>. New York: Viking Studio, 2001.

2. Two or Three Authors

Kress, Gunther, and Theo van Leeuwen. <u>Reading Images: The Grammar of</u>

<u>Graphic Design</u>. London: Routledge, 1996.

3. Four or More Authors

After the first name, add *et al.* ("and others"). If you wish to give all the names, also list them in any in-text citations (see Entry 9, p. 72).

Bellah, Robert N., et al. Habits of the Heart: Individualism and

Commitment in American Life. Berkeley: U of California P, 1985.

4. Organization or Group Author

If the group is the publisher, repeat its name, abbreviated if appropriate.

Nemours Children's Clinic. Diabetes and Me. Wilmington: Nemours, 2001.

5. No Author Given

Guide for Authors. Oxford: Blackwell, 1985.

6. More Than One Work by the Same Author

Tannen, Deborah. The Argument Culture: Moving from Debate to Dialogue.

New York: Random, 1998.

---. You Just Don't Understand: Women and Men in Conversation. New

York: Ballantine, 1991.

7. One or More Editors

Achebe, Chinua, and C. L. Innes, eds. African Short Stories. London:

Heinemann, 1985.

8. Author and Editor

Wardlow, Gayle Dean. Chasin' That Devil Music: Searching for the Blues.

Ed. Edward Komara. San Francisco: Miller, 1998.

9. Translator

Baudrillard, Jean. <u>Cool Memories II: 1978-1990</u>. Trans. Chris Turner.

    Durham: Duke UP, 1996.

10. Edition Following the First

Coe, Michael D. <u>The Maya</u>. 7th ed. New York: Thames, 2005.

11. Reprint

Kerouac, Jack. <u>On the Road</u>. 1957. New York: Viking, 1997.

12. Multivolume Work

You may cite the whole work or a specific volume, ending with the total volumes or the full range of dates.

Tsao, Hsueh-chin. <u>The Story of the Stone</u>. Trans. David Hawkes. 5 vols.

    Harmondsworth, Eng.: Penguin, 1983-86.

Tsao, Hsueh-chin. <u>The Story of the Stone</u>. Trans. David Hawkes. Vol. 1.

    Harmondsworth, Eng.: Penguin, 1983. 5 vols.

13. Work in a Series

Hess, Gary R. <u>Vietnam and the United States: Origins and Legacy of War</u>.

    Intl. Hist. Ser. 7. Boston: Twayne, 1990.

14. Book Pre-1900

Darwin, Charles. <u>Descent of Man and Selection in Relation to Sex</u>.

    New York, 1896.

15. Book with Publisher's Imprint

Give the imprint name, a hyphen, and the publisher's name.

Sikes, Gini. 8 Ball Chicks: A Year in the Violent World of Girl Gangs.

New York: Anchor-Doubleday, 1997.

16. Anthology or Collection of Articles

Wu, Duncan, ed. Romantic Women Poets: An Anthology. Oxford: Blackwell,

1997.

To cite a specific selection, see Entries 35 and 36, page 82.

17. Conference Proceedings

Childhood Obesity: Causes and Prevention. Symposium Proc., 27 Oct.

1998. Washington: Center for Nutrition Policy and Promotion, 1999.

18. Title Within a Title

Weick, Carl F. Refiguring Huckleberry Finn. Athens: U of Georgia P, 2000.

Golden, Catherine, ed. The Captive Imagination: A Casebook on "The

Yellow Wallpaper." New York: Feminist, 1992.

19. Pamphlet

Vareika, William. John La Farge: An American Master (1835-1910).

Newport: Gallery of American Art, 1989.

20. Dissertation Published

Said, Edward W. Joseph Conrad and the Fiction of Autobiography. Diss.

Harvard U, 1964. Cambridge: Harvard UP, 1966.

21. Dissertation Unpublished

Cook, Brian Ray. "Reclamation and Imagination." Diss. U of Colorado at

Denver and Health Sciences Center, 2005.

22. Government Document

Perez, Georgia. <u>Tricky Treats</u>. US Dept. of Health and Human Services.

Centers for Disease Control and Prevention. Washington: GPO, 2006.

United States. Cong. House. <u>Anti-Spamming Act of 2001</u>. 107th Cong., 1st

sess. Washington: GPO, 2001.

23. Sacred Text

<u>Zondervan NIV Study Bible</u>. Grand Rapids: Zondervan, 2006.

Articles from Periodicals and Selections from Books

Provide the author's name (last name first), article title (in quotation marks), book or periodical title (underlined), and publication information (volume number for a periodical, date, page numbers). When the pages are not consecutive, give the first one with a + (48+).

24. Article in Journal Paginated by Volume

When each volume consists of several issues with continuous pagination through them all, supply the volume number.

Eagleton, Terry. "Political Beckett?" <u>New Left Review</u> 40 (2006): 67-74.

25. Article in Journal Paginated by Issue

When each issue begins on page 1, add the issue number after the volume.

Jain, Sarah S. "Violent Submission: Gendered Automobility." <u>Cultural</u>

<u>Critique</u> 61.1 (2005): 186-214.

26. Article in Weekly Magazine

Ripley, Amanda. "Loose Lips." <u>Time</u> 18 June 2007: 15.

27. Article in Monthly Magazine

Zimmer, Carl. "Mendel's Mouse." <u>Discover</u> May 2007: 30-34.

28. Article with No Author Given

"The Obesity Industry." <u>Economist</u> 27 Sept. 2003: 64+.

29. Article in Newspaper

Add the city in brackets after the title unless it is named there.

Willis, Ellen. "Steal This Myth: Why We Still Try to Re-create the

     Rush of the 60's." <u>New York Times</u> 20 Aug. 2000, late ed.,

     sec. 2: AR1+.

30. Editorial

"A False Choice." Editorial. <u>Charlotte Observer</u> 16 Aug. 1998: 2C.

31. Letter to the Editor

Gibson, Blake. Letter. <u>Denver Post</u> 27 June 2007: 6B.

32. Interview Published

Stewart, Martha. "'I Do Have a Brain.'" Interview with Kevin Kelly. <u>Wired</u>

     Aug. 1998: 114.

33. Review

Include the reviewer and the review's title, if available.

Muñoz, José Esteban. "Citizens and Superheroes." Rev. of <u>The Queen of</u>

     <u>America Goes to Washington City</u>, by Lauren Berlant. <u>American</u>

     <u>Quarterly</u> 52 (2000): 397-404.

Hadjor, Kofi Buenor. Rev. of The Silent War: Imperialism and the

   Changing Perception of Race, by Frank Furendi. Journal of Black

   Studies 30 (1999): 133-35.

34. Article in Encyclopedia or Reference Work

Oliver, Paul, and Barry Kernfeld. "Blues." The New Grove Dictionary of

   Jazz. Ed. Barry Kernfeld. New York: St. Martin's, 1994.

"The History of Western Theatre." The New Encyclopaedia Britannica:

   Macropedia. 15th ed. 1987. Vol. 28.

35. Chapter in Edited Book or Selection in Anthology

Atwood, Margaret. "Bluebeard's Egg." "Bluebeard's Egg" and Other Stories.

   New York: Fawcett-Random, 1987. 131-64.

For a reprinted selection, you may add the original source.

Atwood, Margaret. "Bluebeard's Egg." "Bluebeard's Egg" and Other

   Stories. New York: Fawcett-Random, 1987. 131-64. Rpt. in Don't Bet

   on the Prince: Contemporary Feminist Fairy Tales in North America

   and England. Ed. Jack Zipes. New York: Methuen, 1989.160-82.

36. More Than One Selection from Anthology or Collection

Reduce repetition. Identify the collection in one entry; refer to it from entries
for selections.

Goldberg, Jonathan. "Speculation: Macbeth and Source." Howard and

   O'Connor 242-64.

Howard, Jean E., and Marion F. O'Connor, eds. <u>Shakespeare Reproduced:</u>

    <u>The Text in History and Ideology</u>. New York: Methuen, 1987.

37. Preface, Foreword, Introduction, or Afterword

Greven, Philip J. Foreword. <u>Children in Colonial America</u>. Ed. James

    Marten. New York: New York UP, 2007.

38. Letter Published

Garland, Hamlin. "To Fred Lewis Pattee." 30 Dec. 1914. Letter 206

    of <u>Selected Letters of Hamlin Garland</u>. Ed. Keith Newlin and

    Joseph B. McCullough. Lincoln: U of Nebraska P, 1998.

39. Dissertation Abstract

Hawkins, Joanne Berning. "Horror Cinema and the Avante-Garde." Diss. U.

    of California, Berkeley, 1993. <u>DAI</u> 55 (1995): 1712A.

Field and Media Resources

40. Interview Unpublished

Identify the person interviewed and the type of interview: *Personal interview* (you conducted it in person), *Telephone interview* (you talked to the person over the telephone), or *Interview* (someone else conducted the interview, perhaps on radio or television).

Schutt, Robin. E-mail interview. 7 Oct. 2007.

Sedgwick, Kyra. Interview with James Lipton. <u>Inside the Actors Studio</u>.

    Bravo, New York. 11 June 2007.

41. Survey or Questionnaire

MLA doesn't specify a form, but you might cite your field research this way.

Figliozzi, Jennifer Emily, and Summer J. Arrigo-Nelson. Questionnaire on

Student Alcohol Use and Parental Values. U of Rhode Island,

Kingston. 15-20 Apr. 2004.

42. Observation

MLA doesn't specify a form, but you might cite your field notes this way.

Ba, Ed. Ski Run Observation. Vail, CO. 26 Jan. 2007.

43. Letter or Memo Unpublished

Hall, Donald. Letter to the author. 24 Jan. 1990.

44. Oral Presentation

Phillips, Maureen. "Women Veterans: Degendering Patriotism." Conf. on

Coll. Composition and Communication Convention. Hilton New York,

New York. 23 Mar. 2007.

45. Performance

110 in the Shade. By N. Richard Nash. Dir. Lonny Price. Studio 54,

New York. 3 July 2007.

46. Video or Film

Rosencrantz and Guildenstern Are Dead. Dir. Tom Stoppard. Perf. Gary

Oldman, Tim Roth, and Richard Dreyfuss. Videocassette. Buena Vista

Home Video, 1990.

Super Size Me. Prod. Morgan Spurlock. Perf. Morgan Spurlock. Samuel

Goldwyn Films, 2004.

47. Television or Radio Program

"The Tour." I Love Lucy. Dir. William Asher. Nickelodeon. 2 July 2001.

48. Recording

Identify the recording's form unless it's a compact disc.

The Goo-Goo Dolls. Dizzy Up the Girl. Warner, 1998.

Mozart, Wolfgang Amadeus. Symphony no. 40 in G minor. Vienna

Philharmonic. Cond. Leonard Bernstein. Audiocassette. Deutsche

Grammophon, 1984.

49. Artwork or Photograph

Leonardo da Vinci. Mona Lisa. Louvre, Paris.

Larimer Street, Denver. Personal photograph by author. 5 May 2007.

50. Map or Chart

Arkansas. Map. Comfort, TX: Gousha, 1996.

51. Comic Strip or Cartoon

Cochran, Tony. "Agnes." Comic Strip. Denver Post 18 Apr. 2007: 13F.

52. Advertisement

Toyota. Advertisement. GQ July 2001: 8.

Online and Electronic Resources

For each entry supply the date when the material was published in print
(if any), posted (or last updated), and accessed by you. Note the address
or URL (beginning with *http, gopher, telnet, ftp*) in angle brackets. Include
the search page, links, path, or file name needed for a reader to reach the
page you used. Break a URL only after a slash (without adding a hyphen).

53. Web Site

<u>Cartoon America</u>. 21 Nov. 2006. Lib. of Congress. 18 Apr. 2007

    <http://www.loc.gov/exhibits/cartoonamerica>.

54. Academic Home Page

Baron, Dennis. Home page. Dept. of English, U of Illinois, Urbana-

    Champaign. 18 Apr. 2007 <http://www.english.uiuc.edu/

    -people-/faculty/baron/.html>.

55. Course Home Page

Jolly, Jennifer. Arts in the Americas. Course home page. 18 Jan.-3 May

    2006. Art History Dept., Ithaca College. 11 May 2007 <http://

    www.ithaca.edu/faculty/jjolly/americas/>.

56. Blog

Adapt a similar format for a new source, such as a blog.

Ramsey, Doug. "Zoot, Red, Lorraine." Weblog posting. <u>Rifftides</u>. 5 Mar.

    2007. 10 Mar. 2007 <http://www.artsjournal.com/rifftides/>.

57. Podcast

Adapt a similar format for a new source, such as a podcast.

"You Are Getting Sleepy. . . ." <u>The Loh Down on Science</u>. Perf. Sandra

    Tsing Loh. 12 Mar. 2007. Natl. Public Radio. KPCC, Pasadena.

    14 Mar. 2007 <http://www.scpr.org/programs/perspectives/

    lohscience.html>.

58. Book: Online

London, Jack. The Iron Heel. New York: Macmillan, 1908. The Jack London

Collection. 25 July 2006. Berkeley Digital Lib. SunSITE. 18 Apr. 2007

<http://london.sonoma.edu/Writings/IronHeel>.

59. Selection from Book: Online

Muir, John. "The City of the Saints." Steep Trails. 1918. 17 Apr. 2007

<http://encyclopediaindex.com/b/sttrl10.htm>.

60. Journal Article: Online

Dugdale, Timothy. "The Fan and (Auto)Biography: Writing the Self in the

Stars." Journal of Mundane Behavior 1.2 (2000). 19 Apr. 2007

<http://www.mundanebehavior.org/issues/v1n2/dugdale.htm>.

61. Magazine Article: Online

Wright, Laura. "My, What Big Eyes . . ." Discover 27 Oct. 2003. 14 July

2007 <http://discovermagazine.com/>.

62. Newspaper Article: Online

Mulvihill, Kim. "Childhood Obesity." San Francisco Chronicle 12 July 2001.

15 Oct. 2006 <http://www.sfgate.com/search>.

63. Government Document: Online

United States. Dept. of Commerce. Bureau of the Census. Census Brief:

Disabilities Affect One-Fifth of All Americans. Dec. 1997. 18 July 2006

<http://www.census.gov/prod/3/97pubs/cenbr975.pdf>.

64. Editorial: Online

"Mall Mania/A Measure of India's Success." Editorial. <u>StarTribune.com</u>

Minneapolis-St. Paul 31 Oct. 2003. 14 Nov. 2006 <http://

www.startribune.com/stories/1519/4185511.html>.

65. Letter to the Editor: Online

Taylor, Ralph. Letter. <u>Denverpost.com</u> June 2007. 30 June 2007

<http://www.denverpost.com/opinion/ci_6263554>.

66. Interview: Online

Rikker, David. Interview with Victor Payan. <u>San Diego Latino</u>

<u>Film Festival</u>. May 1999. 20 Jan. 2007 <http://www.sdlatinofilm.com/

video.html#Anchor-David-64709>.

67. Review: Online

Chaudhury, Parama. Rev. of <u>Kandahar</u>, dir. Mohsen Makhmalbaf. <u>Film</u>

<u>Monthly</u> 3.4 (2002). 19 Jan. 2007. <http://www.filmmonthly.com/

Playing/Articles/Kandahar/Kandahar.html>.

68. Abstract: Online

Schwitzer, Alan M., and Laura Hinsley Choate. "College Student Needs and

Counseling Responses." <u>Journal of College Counseling</u> 10.1 (2007).

Abstract. 29 June 2007 <http://www.counseling.org/journals/

jccspr207.htm#schwitzer>.

69. Journal Article: Online Database

Reger, Jo. "Where Are the Leaders? Music, Culture, and Contemporary

   Feminism." <u>American Behavioral Scientist</u> 50 (2007): 1350-69.

   <u>Electronic Journals Service</u>. EBSCOhost. Auraria Lib., Denver, CO. 29

   June 2007 <http://0-ejournals.ebsco.com.skyline.cudenver.edu/

   Home.asp>.

70. Article Abstract: Online Database

Sofaer, Abraham D. "Presidential Power and National Security."

   <u>Presidential Studies Quarterly</u> 37 (2007): 101-. Abstract.

   <u>InfoTrac OneFile</u>. Thomson Gale. Auraria Lib., Denver, CO.

   29 June 2007 <http://0-find.galegroup.com.skyline.cudenver.edu/>.

71. Magazine Article: Online Database

Barrett, Jennifer. "Fast Food Need Not Be Fat Food." <u>Newsweek</u> 13 Oct.

   2003: 73-74. <u>Academic Search Premier</u>. EBSCOhost. U of Rhode Island

   Lib. 31 Oct. 2003 <http://0-ejournals.ebsco.com>.

72. Newspaper Article: Online Database

Lee, R. "Class with the 'Ph.D. Diva.'" <u>New York Times</u> 18 Oct. 2003: B7.

   <u>InfoTrac OneFile</u>. Thomson Gale. Providence Public Lib., RI. 31 Oct.

   2006 <http://infotrac.galegroup.com/menu>.

Journal Article from a Subscription Database (HTML Format)

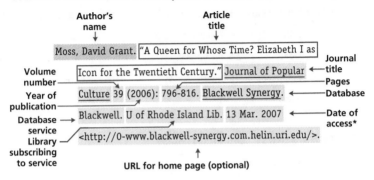

Author's name → Moss, David Grant.

Article title → "A Queen for Whose Time? Elizabeth I as Icon for the Twentieth Century."

Journal title → Journal of Popular

Volume number → Culture 39

Year of publication → (2006):

Pages → 796-816.

Database → Blackwell Synergy.

Database service → Blackwell.

Library subscribing to service → U of Rhode Island Lib.

Date of access* → 13 Mar. 2007

URL for home page (optional) → <http://0-www.blackwell-synergy.com.helin.uri.edu/>.

*For date of access, use the date you visited the source.

Database **URL**

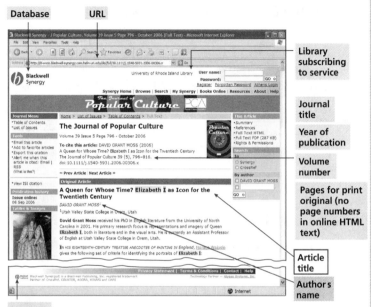

Library subscribing to service

Journal title

Year of publication

Volume number

Pages for print original (no page numbers in online HTML text)

Article title

Author's name

Database service

Journal Article from a Subscription Database (PDF Format)

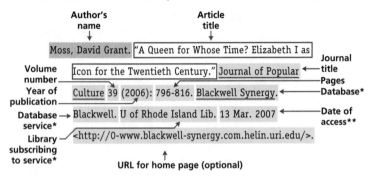

*Database, database service, and library subscribing to service are not provided in the .pdf version. Obtain this information from the database screen.

**For date of access, use the date you visited the source.

URL →

Labels in left margin:

Article title →

Author's name →

Journal title

Volume number →

Year of publication

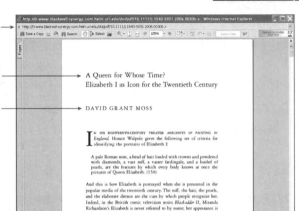

Screen content:

A Queen for Whose Time?
Elizabeth I as Icon for the Twentieth Century

DAVID GRANT MOSS

I N HIS EIGHTEENTH-CENTURY TREATISE *ANECDOTES OF PAINTING IN England,* Horace Walpole gives the following set of criteria for identifying the portraits of Elizabeth I:

A pale Roman nose, a head of hair loaded with crowns and powdered with diamonds, a vast ruff, a vaster fardingale, and a bushel of pearls, are the features by which every body knows at once the pictures of Queen Elizabeth. (150)

And this is how Elizabeth is portrayed when she is presented in the popular media of the twentieth century. The ruff, the hair, the pearls, and the elaborate dresses are the cues by which people recognize her. Indeed, in the British comic television series *Blackadder II,* Miranda Richardson's Elizabeth is never referred to by name; her appearance is more than enough to indicate who she is.

Richardson's appearance, like that of so many other screen Elizabeths, is that of the Ditchley portrait (which fits Walpole's description particularly well). The Ditchley portrait (Figure 1) has in effect become the standard image of her in popular culture. In Shekhar Kapur's film *Elizabeth (1998),* the film ends with Elizabeth transformed by wig, makeup, and costume into a stiff, pale, statuesque icon in white; Kapur's Elizabeth becomes the Ditchley painting even though the film purports to end in 1563, almost thirty years before the painting was completed.[1]

The Journal of Popular Culture, Vol. 39, No. 5, 2006
© 2006, Copyright the Authors
Journal compilation © 2006, Blackwell Publishing, Inc.

796

73. Summary of Research: Online Database

Holub, Tamara. "Early-Decision Programs." ERIC Digests. ERIC: Educational
  Resources Information Center. ED470540. 2002. Auraria Lib., Denver, CO.
  30 June 2007 <http://www.eric.ed.gov/ERICWebPortal/Home.portal>.

74. Collection of Documents: Online Database

"Combating Plagiarism." CQ Researcher 9 Sept. 2003. CQ P. U of Rhode Island
  Lib. 12 Nov. 2006 <http://0-library.cqpress.com.helin.uri. edu:80/
  cqresearcher/>.

75. Personal Subscription Service: Online Database

Introduce your access route by *Keyword* or *Path.*

"Native American Food Guide." Health Finder. 16 July 2001. America
  Online. 16 July 2006. Keyword: Health.

76. Video or Film: Online

Coppola, Francis Ford, dir. Apocalypse Now. 1979. Film.com. 17 July 2006
  <http://ramhurl.film.com/smildemohurl.ram?file=screen/2001/clips/
  apoca.smi>.

77. Television or Radio Program: Online

Kuhn, Anthony. "China's Workforce Gets Rights." Morning Edition.
  Natl. Public Radio. 29 June 2007. 17 July 2007 <http://www.npr.org/>.

78. Recording: Online

Malcolm X. "The Ballot or the Bullet." 12 Apr. 1964. Malcolm. 30 June 2007
  <http://www.brothermalcolm.net/index.html>.

79. Artwork: Online

Winged Victory of Samothrace. c. 190 BC. Louvre, Paris. 6 July 2007

    <http://www.louvre.fr/llv/commun/home_flash.jsp>.

80. Map or Chart: Online

"Beirut [Beyrout] 1912." Map. Perry-Castañeda Library Map Collection. 1 July

    2007 <http://www.lib.utexas.edu/maps/historical/beirut2_1912. jpg>.

81. Comic Strip or Cartoon: Online

Auth, Tony. "Spending Goals." Cartoon. Slate 7 Sept. 2001. 16 Oct. 2006

    <http://cagle.slate.msn.com/politicalcartoons/pccartoons/archives/

    auth.asp>.

82. Advertisement: Online

Mazda Miata. Advertisement. 16 July 2001 <http://www.mazdausa.com/miata/>.

83. Other Online Sources

When citing an electronic source not explained here, adapt the appropriate
nonelectronic MLA model.

NASA/JPL. "Martian Meteorite." Views of the Solar System: Meteoroids

    and Meteorites. Ed. Calvin J. Hamilton. 1999. 13 June 2005

    <http://spaceart.com/solar/eng/meteor.htm#views>.

84. FTP, Telnet, or Gopher Site

Treat a source obtained through FTP (file transfer protocol), telnet, or gopher
as you would a similar Web source.

Clinton, William Jefferson. "Radio Address of the President to the Nation."

    10 May 1997. 29 June 2003 <ftp://OMA.EOP.GOV.US/1997/5/10/1.TEXT.1>.

85. Email

Give the writer's name, the title (or type) of communication, and the date.

Pell, John. "City Board." E-mail to the author. 17 Sept. 2006.

86. Online Posting

Aid readers (if you can) by citing an archived version.

Brock, Stephen E. "School Crisis." Online posting. 27 Apr. 2001. Special

Events Chat Transcripts. Lycos Communities. 18 July 2006 <http://

clubs.lycos.com/live/Events/transcripts/school_crisis_tscript.asp>.

87. Synchronous Communication

For a MUD, a MOO, or another form of synchronous communication, identify the speaker, the event, its date, its forum (CollegeTownMOO, for instance), your access date, and the address. Cite an archived version if possible.

Finch, Jeremy. Online debate "Can Proust Save Your Life?" 3 Apr. 1998.

CollegeTownMOO. 3 Apr. 1998 <telnet://next.cs.bvc.edu.7777>.

88. CD-ROM, Diskette, or Magnetic Tape

Shakespeare, William. All's Well That Ends Well. William Shakespeare: The

Complete Works on CD-ROM. CD-ROM. Abingdon, Eng.: Andromeda

Interactive, 1994.

89. CD-ROM Abstract

Straus, Stephen. Interview with Claudia Dreifus. "Separating Remedies

from Snake Oil." New York Times 3 Apr. 2001: D5+. Abstract. CD-ROM.

InfoTrac. 19 July 2006.

17c MLA sample pages

First page

1" from top

↕ ¹/₂" from top

Latimer 1

Jenny Latimer   **Heading format without title page**   **1" margin on each side**

Professor Schwegler

Writing 101   **Double-spaced heading and paper**

7 November 2006

¶ indented 5 spaces or ¹/₂"   No, Thanks, I'll Pass on That   **Title centered**

1   One night at work my friend Kate turned down my offer of a red licorice stick after quickly checking the ingredients on the bag. I asked her to explain why, and she replied that they contained hydrogenated oils, which are, according to research articles she had read, "silent killers." She went on briefly to describe the horrors they do to your body, the various foods that contain them, as well as the effort she makes to avoid hydrogenated oils. I was shocked and intrigued by this news and decided to explore the reality of what she'd said.

2   My first question was this: what exactly does it mean to hydrogenate an oil? This is where things get a little technical: to hydrogenate is to add hydrogen. During the hydrogenation process, the hydrogen atoms of a fatty acid are moved to the opposite side of the double bond of its molecular structure (Roberts). According to Lewis Harrison, author of The Complete Fats and Oils Book, this changed fatty acid molecule can actually be toxic to the body. It can cause oxidative stress and damage the body in the same way as cigarette smoke and chemical toxins. . . .

Paper continues, investigating questions about hydrogenated fats

Begin on new page

Sources listed
alphabetically

1" from top

Works Cited   Heading centered

Page
numbers
continue

American Heart Association. "Hydrogenated Fats." 2002. 26 Oct. 2006

<http://www.amhrt.org/presenter.jhtml?identifier=4662>.

Armstrong. Eric. "What's Wrong with Partially Hydrogenated Oils?" <u>Treelight</u>

<u>Health.com</u>. 2001. 30 Sept. 2006 <http://www.treelight.com/health/

PartiallyHydrogenatedOils.html>.

Harrison, Lewis. <u>The Complete Fats and Oils Book</u>. New York: Avery-Penguin, 1996.

Marshall, James R. "Trans Fatty Acids in Cancer." <u>Nutrition Reviews</u> May 1996.

Abstract. <u>Health & Wellness Resource Center</u>. Thomson Gale. U of

Rhode Island Lib. 26 Oct. 2006 <http://galenet.galegroup.com>.

Roberts, Shauna S. "IOM Takes Aims at Trans Fats." <u>Diabetes Forecast</u> 56

(2003): 17-18. <u>Academic Search Premier</u>. EBSCOhost. U of Rhode Island

Lib. 26 Oct. 2006 <http://0-web20.epnet.com>.

Rudin, Donald, and Clara Felix. <u>The Omega-3 Phenomenon</u>. New York: Rawson

Assoc., 1987.

"Think Before You Eat: Trans Fats Lurking in Many Popular Foods." <u>Knight</u>

<u>Ridder/Tribune News Service</u> 8 Sept. 2003. <u>InfoTrac OneFile</u>. Thomson Gale.

Providence Public Lib., RI. 26 Oct. 2006 <http://web4.infotrac.galegroup.com>.

United States. Food and Drug Administration. "What Every Consumer Should

Know About Trans Fatty Acids." 9 July 2003. 23 Oct. 2006 <http://

www.fda.gov/oc/initiatives/transfat/q_a.html>.

Additional
lines
indented
5 spaces
or ¹/₂"

GUIDE TO APA FORMATS

APA Formats for In-Text (Parenthetical) Citations

APA Formats for References

(continued)

18 | APA Style

　　The APA (American Psychological Association) documentation style uses the author's name and the date of publication—within parentheses or in the text—to identify a source. This in-text citation guides readers to a detailed entry in a reference list at the end of the paper.

Use this "name-and-date" style when you write in a social science field or in a workplace or public setting where readers prefer a name-and-date system or want to see immediately how current your sources are. For more on APA style, consult the *Publication Manual of the American Psychological Association* (5th ed., Washington, DC: APA, 2001) or updates posted on the APA Web site: <http://www.apastyle.org>.

18a APA in-text (parenthetical) citations

In APA style, you generally use parentheses in the text to enclose references to your sources. Include author and date, separated by a comma, unless you have mentioned the author's name in your discussion.

1. Author's Name in Parentheses

IN PARENTHESES   As stars and fans go online, studies of their interactions

continue (Gitlin, 2001).

2. Author's Name in Discussion

IN DISCUSSION   Gitlin (2001) found that emotion bonds fan and celebrity.

3. Specific Reference

Specify the location of a quotation, paraphrase, or summary by adding p. or pp. and the page or pages in the source. Spell out the word *figure*.

QUOTATION   A recent study examined the emotional intensity of "the

fan's link to the star" (Gitlin, 2001, p. 129).

4. Specific Reference to Online Source

Use what the document provides: page numbers, paragraph numbers (para. or ¶), or the section name and paragraph under it, counted to number.

Bodybuilders sometimes suffer from muscle dysmorphia (Lee, 2006,

What is dysmorphia? section, para. 4).

5. One Author

Dell's 2006 report on charter schools confirmed trends identified earlier

(James, 1996) and updated Rau's classification (1998).

6. Two Authors

Include both names. Separate them with an ampersand (&) in parenthetical citations; in your text, use *and*.

Given evidence that married men earn more than unmarried men (Chun

& Lee, 2001), Nakosteen and Zimmer (2001) investigated how earnings

affect spousal selection.

7. Three to Five Authors

For the first citation, include all the names, separated by commas with *and* in the text or an ampersand (&) in parentheses.

Sadeh, Raviv, and Gruber (2000) related "sleep problems and

neuropsychological functioning in children" (p. 292).

In any subsequent references, use the first author's name with *et al.* ("and others"): Sadeh et al. (2000) reported their findings.

8. Six or More Authors

In text citations, follow the first author's name with *et al.* (Berg et al., 1998). (See Entry 2, p. 105.)

9. Organization or Group Author

Spell out the name of the association, corporation, or agency in the first citation. Follow any cumbersome name with an abbreviation in brackets so you can use the shorter form in later citations.

FIRST CITATION   Besides instilling fear, hate crimes limit where women live and

work (National Organization of Women [NOW], 2001).

LATER CITATION   Pending legislation would strengthen the statutes on bias-

motivated crimes (NOW, 2001).

10. No Author Given

Give the title or the first few words of a long title.

These photographs reveal similarity in variety (*Friendship*, 2001).

Full title: *Friendship: Celebration of humanity.*

11. Authors with the Same Name

Add initials to distinguish authors with the same last name.

Studies of African American culture during slavery (E. Foner, 1988)

often cited Frederick Douglass (P. Foner, 1950).

12. Work Cited More Than Once

When you cite the same source again in a paragraph, repeat the citation to clarify a page or specify one of several sources. If a second reference is clear, don't repeat the date.

Much increased personal debt can be linked to use of credit cards

(Schor, 1998, p. 73). In fact, according to Schor, roughly a third of

consumers are "either heavily or moderately in financial debt" (p. 72).

13. Two or More Sources in a Citation

If you sum up several sources, list them all in your citation. Arrange them alphabetically, then oldest to most recent for works by the same author.

Several studies have related job satisfaction and performance (Faire,

2002; Hall, 1996, 2001).

14. Two or More Works by the Same Author in the Same Year

Alphabetize works published in the same year by the same author or author team, and add letters after the year to distinguish them.

Gould (1987a, p. 73) makes a similar point.

15. Work Cited in Another Source

Writing in the late 1800s about Halloween customs, Walsh lamented

that "gangs of hoodlums throng the streets, ringing the door-bells"

(as cited in Skal, 2002, pp. 33-34).

16. Sacred or Classical Text

Give the number or name of the chapter, section, or part along with the date or name of the version, especially if no original date is available. Cite a standard source in your text only.

Aristotle argues in *Politics* (trans. 1999) that liberty is a fundamental

element of democracy (6.1.6).

17. Personal Communications, Including Interviews and Email

Cite letters, memos, interviews, email, telephone conversations, and similar sources using the person's name, the phrase *personal communication,* and the full date. Omit these sources from your reference list.

According to J. M. Hostos, the state no longer funds services duplicated

by county agencies (personal communication, October 7, 2007).

18. Content Footnote

You may use a content footnote to expand on material. In the text add a superscript number, placed slightly above the related line of text. On a new page at the end, below the centered heading "Footnotes," present the notes in consecutive numerical order, as in the text. Indent a half inch (five to seven spaces) for the initial line in each note, and double-space all notes.

TEXT   I tape-recorded and transcribed all interviews.[1]

NOTE   [1]Although background noise obscured some parts of the

                tapes, these gaps did not substantially affect the study.

18b APA reference list

Your list of sources lets readers identify and consult what you cite.

- Begin the list with the centered title "References" on a new page at the end of your text but before appendixes or notes. (See p. 121.)
- List your sources alphabetically by author (or title if there is no author), then oldest to most recent for those by the same author.
- Do not indent the first line of each entry; indent the rest of the entry in paragraph style, a half inch or five to seven spaces.
- Double-space the entire list. Leave a single space after a period in an entry (except in abbreviations such as U.S.).

Books and Works Treated as Books

Include the last name of each author, a comma, and *initials only* for first and middle names; year of publication in parentheses; title (capitalizing only the first word, the subtitle's first word, and proper names); city of publication (with the country or the state's postal abbreviation, except for major cities); and publisher's name, with *Press* or *Books* but not *Inc.* or *Publishers*.

1. One Author

Wilson, W. J. (1996). *When work disappears: The world of the new urban*

   poor. New York, Knopf.

2. Two or More Authors

List up to six authors; add *et al.* to show others: Nu, P., et al. . . .

Biber, D., Conrad, S., & Reppen, R. (1998). *Corpus linguistics: Investigating language structure and use*. Cambridge, England: Cambridge University Press.

3. Organization or Group Author

Treat the group as author. When author and publisher are the same, use *Author* after the place instead of repeating the name.

Amnesty International. (2003). *Annual report 2003*. London: Author.

4. No Author Given

Boas anniversary volume: Anthropological papers written in honor of Franz Boas. (1906). New York: Stechert.

5. More Than One Work by the Same Author

List works chronologically.

Aronowitz, S. (1993). *Roll over Beethoven: The return of cultural strife*. Hanover, NH: Wesleyan University Press.

Aronowitz, S. (2000). *From the ashes of the old: American labor and America's future*. New York: Basic Books.

6. More Than One Work by the Same Author in the Same Year

Gould, S. J. (1987a). *Time's arrow, time's cycle: Myth and metaphor in the discovery of geological time*. Cambridge, MA: Harvard University Press.

Gould, S. J. (1987b). *An urchin in the storm: Essays about books and ideas*. New York: Norton.

7. One or More Editors

Bowe, J., Bowe, M., & Streeter, S. C. (Eds.). (2001). *Gig: Americans talk about their jobs*. New York: Three Rivers Press.

8. Translator

Bourdieu, P. (1990). *In other words: Essays towards a reflexive sociology* (M. Adamson, Trans.). Stanford, CA: Stanford University Press.

9. Edition Following the First

Groth-Marnat, G. (2003). *Handbook of psychological assessment* (4th ed.). New York: Wiley.

10. Reprint

Butler, J. (1999). *Gender trouble*. New York: Routledge. (Original work published 1990)

11. Multivolume Work

Strachey, J., Freud, A., Strachey, A., & Tyson, A. (Eds.). (1966-1974). *The standard edition of the complete psychological works of Sigmund Freud* (J. Strachey et al., Trans.) (Vols. 3-5). London: Hogarth Press and the Institute of Psycho-Analysis.

12. Anthology or Collection of Articles

Appadurai, A. (Ed.). (2001). *Globalization*. Durham, NC: Duke University Press.

13. Encyclopedia or Reference Work

Winn, P. (Ed.). (2001). *Dictionary of biological psychology*. London: Routledge.

14. *Diagnostic and Statistical Manual of Mental Disorders*

After a full in-text citation for this manual, use these abbreviations: *DSM-III* (1980), *DSM-III-R* (1987), *DSM-IV* (1994), or *DSM-IV-TR* (2000).

American Psychiatric Association. (1994). *Diagnostic and statistical manual*

of mental disorders (4th ed.). Washington, DC: Author.

15. Dissertation Unpublished

Gomes, C. S. (2001). *Selection and treatment effects in managed care.*

Unpublished doctoral dissertation, Boston University.

16. Government Document

Committee on Energy and Natural Resources, Senate. (2007). *Alaska Water*

Resources Act of 2007 (Com. Rep. No. 110-020). Washington, DC: U.S.

Government Printing Office.

17. Report

Dossey, J. A. (1988). *Mathematics: Are we measuring up?* (Report No.

17-M-02). Princeton, NJ: Educational Testing Service. (ERIC Document

Reproduction Service No. ED300207)

Articles from Periodicals and Selections from Books

For an article, provide the following: author's name (last name first); date (in parentheses); title (without quotation marks, capitalizing only the first word of the title and subtitle and proper names); journal title (in italics, capitalizing all main words), volume number (in italics), and page numbers.

18. Article in Journal Paginated by Volume

Klein, R. D. (2003). Audience reactions to local TV news. *American Behavioral Scientist, 46*, 1661-1672.

19. Article in Journal Paginated by Issue

Sadeh, A., Raviv, A., & Gruber, R. (2000). Sleep patterns and sleep disruptions in school-age children. *Developmental Psychology, 36*(3), 291-301.

20. Article in Weekly Magazine

Kluger, J. (2007, June 11). The science of appetite. *Time, 169*, 48-52, 57-58, 61.

21. Article in Monthly Magazine

Dold, C. (1998, September). Needles and nerves. *Discover, 19*, 59-62.

22. Article in Newspaper

Raabe, S. (2007, June 26). High wattage, low outages. *The Denver Post*, pp. 1C, 4C.

23. Editorial or Letter to the Editor

Ellis, S. (2001, September 7). Adults are problem with youth sports [Letter to the editor]. *USA Today*, p. A14.

24. Interview Published

APA does not specify a form, but you might use this one.

Dess, N. K. (2001). The new body-mind connection (John T. Cacioppo) [Interview]. *Psychology Today, 34*(4), 30-31.

25. Review with Title

Mack, A. (2007). Consumption nation [Review of the book *Sold American: Consumption and citizenship, 1890-1945*]. *Reviews in American History, 35*, 253-259.

26. Review Without Title

Verdery, K. (2002). [Review of the book *The politics of gender after socialism*]. *American Anthropologist, 104*, 354-355.

27. Article in Encyclopedia or Reference Work

Chernoff, H. (1978). Decision theory. In *International encyclopedia of statistics* (Vol. 1, pp. 131-135). New York: Free Press.

28. Chapter in Edited Book or Selection in Anthology

Chisholm, J. S. (1999). Steps to an evolutionary ecology of mind. In A. L. Hinton (Ed.), *Biocultural approaches to the emotions* (pp. 117-150). Cambridge, England: Cambridge University Press.

29. Dissertation Abstract

Yamada, H. (1989). American and Japanese topic management strategies in business conversations. *Dissertation Abstracts International, 50* (09), 2982B. (UMI No. 9004751)

Field and Media Resources

30. Unpublished Raw Data

Briefly describe field data in brackets; end with *Unpublished raw data.*

Salvo, J. (2007). [Survey of new staff]. Unpublished raw data.

31. Interview Unpublished

Cite your interview of someone only in the text. (See Entry 17, p. 104.)

32. Personal Communications Including Email

Cite letters, email, phone calls, and other communications that cannot be consulted by your readers only in the text. (See Entry 17, p. 104.)

33. Paper Presented at a Meeting

Kisiel, J. F. (2007, April). *Who learns what?* Paper presented at the annual

meeting of the American Educational Research Association, Chicago.

34. Video or Film

Musen, K. (Producer/Writer), & Zimbardo, P. (Writer). (1990). *Quiet rage:*

The Stanford prison study [DVD]. (Available from Insight Media, 2162

Broadway, New York, NY 10024-0621)

35. Television or Radio Program

Siceloff, J. L. (Executive Producer). (2002). *Now with Bill Moyers*

[Television series]. New York: WNET.

36. Recording

Freeman, R. (1994). Porscha [Recorded by R. Freeman & The Rippingtons].

On *Sahara* [CD]. New York: GRP Records.

Online and Electronic Resources

The APA Web site explains new formats for electronic sources (<www .apastyle.org/elecmedia.html>) based on changes in the 2007 *APA Style Guide to Electronic Sources,* available online and highlighted here.

- Give both volume and issue numbers for journal articles.
- Replace a URL with a DOI (Digital Object Identifier) when a publisher has assigned this number to an article or text.
- Note that an item is retrieved from its sponsor or publisher if that identification isn't otherwise clear.
- Name the database (without its URL) for a source that a reader would have trouble finding; otherwise, omit the database.
- Give only the home or menu page URL for a site with full-text subscriptions, references such as encyclopedias, or divisions (frames) that share the same address.
- Note your date of access for online sources subject to revision; omit this date for sources, such as articles, with stable content.

37. Web Site

Brown, D. K. (2001). *The children's literature Web guide*. Retrieved from

http://www.ucalgary.ca/~dkbrown/

38. Blog

Baron, D. (2006, October 26). I found it on Wikipedia, the eBay for

facts. Message posted to http://webtools.uiuc.edu/blog

/view?blogId=25

39. Podcast

Malakoff, D. (Producer). (2007, April 30). Your questions: Carbon

power. *Climate connections*. Podcast retrieved from http://

www.npr.org/

40. Book or Document: Online

If you can't find a publication date, use *n.d.* ("no date").

Frary, R. B. (n.d.). *A brief guide to questionnaire development.* Retrieved

June 30, 2007, from http://ericae.net/ft/tamu/vpiques3.htm

41. Selection from Book or Document: Online

Lasswell, H. D. (1971). Professional training. In *A pre-view of policy sciences*

(chap. 8). Retrieved from http://www.policysciences.org/

42. Journal Article: Online

Wynd, C. A. (2006). A proposed model for military disaster nursing.

OJIN: The Online Journal of Issues in Nursing, 11(3). Retrieved

from http://www.nursingworld.org/ojin/topic31/tpc31_4.htm

43. Journal Article with DOI: Online

Abrahms, M. (2006). Why terrorism does not work. *International Security,*

31(2), 42-78. doi: 10.1162/isec.2006.31.2.42

44. Newsletter Article: Online

Cashel, J. (2007, January 23). Community metrics. *Online Community*

Report. Retrieved from http://www.onlinecommunityreport.com

/archives/134-Community-Metrics.html

45. Newspaper Article: Online

Dortch, D. T. (2007, April 19). Make a start in public service. *Washington*

Post Online. Retrieved from http://www.washingtonpost.com

46. Organization or Agency Document: Online

Arizona Public Health Association. (2006). *AzPHA annual report 2006.*

Retrieved from http://www.azpha.org/

47. Government Document: Online

U.S. Department of Labor, Women's Bureau. (2007). *Women in the labor*

force in 2006. Retrieved from http://www.dol.gov/wb/factsheets

/Qf-laborforce-06.htm

48. Document from Academic Site: Online

Academic programs. (2007). Retrieved from Claremont Graduate University

Web site: http://www.cgu.edu/pages/441.asp

49. Report: Online

Greenpeace International. (2007). *Green guide to electronics.* 4th ed.

Retrieved from http://www.greenpeace.org/international

/press/reports

50. Report from Academic Site: Online

Note "Available from," not "Retrieved from," for a page with directions for accessing a source.

Bartfeld, J., & David, C. (2003). *Food insecurity in Wisconsin,*

1996-2000. (Special Report No. 86). Available from University of

Wisconsin-Madison, Institute for Research on Poverty Web site:

http://www.irp.wisc.edu/publications/specreports.htm

51. Abstract: Online

Abrahms, M. (2006). Why terrorism does not work. *International Security,*
31(2), 42-78. Abstract retrieved from http://www.mitpressjournals.org
/doi/abs/10.1162/isec.2006.31.2.42

52. Journal Article: Online Database

Piko, B. (2001). Gender differences and similarities in adolescents' ways of
coping. *Psychological Record, 51*(2), 223-235.

53. Newspaper Article: Online Database

Sappenfield, M. (2002, June 24). New laws curb teen sports drugs. *The*
Christian Science Monitor. Retrieved from America's Newspapers
database.

54. Presentation from Conference: Online

Wolfram, S. (2006, June 16). *The state of NKS in 2006* [Audio file].
Keynote address at the meeting of the NKS 2006 Wolfram Science
Conference. Retrieved from the Wolfram Science Web site:
http://www.wolframscience.com/conference/2006/presentations/

55. Email

Cite email only in your text. (See Entry 17, p. 104.)

Journal Article from a Subscription Database

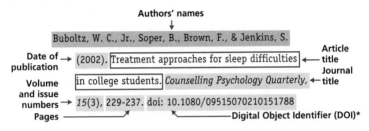

Authors' names
↓

Buboltz, W. C., Jr., Soper, B., Brown, F., & Jenkins, S.

Date of publication → (2002). Treatment approaches for sleep difficulties ← Article title

in college students. *Counselling Psychology Quarterly,* ← Journal title

Volume and issue numbers → *15*(3), 229-237. doi: 10.1080/09515070210151788

Pages ───→   ↖───── Digital Object Identifier (DOI)*

*Supply the article's DOI when available. Unless the source is hard to find, leave out the name of the database containing it (Academic Search Premier, in this example) and its URL. Because this article is stable, not a draft in process, no date of access is needed.

56. Online Posting

Lanbehn, K. (2001, May 9). Effective rural outreach. Message posted to

State Independent Living Council Discussion Newsgroup, archived at

http://www.acils.com/silc/

57. Computer Program

Begin with the author with rights to a program or with its title.

Family Tree Maker (Version 16.0) [Software]. (2006). Fremont, CA:

Learning Company.

For the Digital Object Identifier (DOI), check the search page or the first page of the article.

58. CD-ROM Database

Hall, Edward T. (1998). In *Current biography: 1940-1997*. Retrieved from

Wilson database.

18c APA sample pages

Title page

Number title page and all
others using short title   Body Esteem   1

Running head: BODY ESTEEM   Abbreviate title
(50 characters
maximum) for
running head

Center title   Body Esteem in Women and Men
and all other
lines   Sharon Salamone   Supply name
                                                       and institution
                      University of Rhode Island

                     Professor Robert Schwegler   Supply course
                                                        information and date
                             Writing 233   if requested by your
                                                       instructor
                             Section 2

                          April 30, 2003

Begin on new page

Do not indent   **Center heading**   Abstract

Undergraduate students, male and female, were asked to complete a Body **Double-space abstract and paper** Esteem Survey to report attitudes toward their bodies (body images). Responses to the survey provided an answer to the question of whether the men or the women had higher body esteem. The mean responses for women and men indicated a higher level of body esteem among men with a statistically significant difference in the means. Because the sample was limited to college undergraduates and displayed little variety in ethnicity (predominantly **Summarize paper in one ¶, no more than 120 words** White), the findings of the study are limited. Prior research on ethnicity and body image suggests that a more ethnically varied sample might produce different results.

Besides the abstract, typical sections in an APA paper are an introduction, Method, Results, and Discussion

Begin on new page

Indent ¶s consistently ½" or 5 to 7 spaces

1" from top

Body Esteem   3

Body Esteem in Men and Women   **Title centered**

1   The concept of beauty has changed over the years in Western society, especially for women. In past centuries the ideal was a voluptuous and curved body; now it is a more angular and thin shape (Monteath & McCabe, 1997). Lean, muscular bodies are currently held up as ideals for men, too. Based on such ideals of physical appearance, people considered attractive may be preferred as working partners, as dating partners, or as job candidates (Lennon, Lillethun, & Buckland, 1999). Media images endorse particular body ideals as well; for example, "media in Western countries have portrayed a steadily thinning female body ideal" (Monteath & McCabe, 1997, p. 711).

1" margin on each side

2   Most of us assume that women are quite concerned about their weight and appearance--their body images--and that they often lack positive body esteem, perhaps as a result of media images and other cultural influences (Polivy & Herman, 1987; Rodin, Silberstein, & Striegel-Moore, 1984). But what about men? Is their level of body esteem higher or lower than women's or about the same? In this paper I report on a study I undertook with a group of college undergraduates to compare the attitudes of men and women toward their bodies. In particular, I wanted to determine whether or not the men had a higher body esteem than the women had.

Paper continues with study   **1" margin at bottom**

Begin on new page

**Do not indent
first line**   References

Demarest, J., & Allen, R. (2000). Body image: Gender, ethnic, and age

     differences. *Journal of Social Psychology, 140*, 465-471.

Lennon, S. J., Lillethun, A., & Buckland, S. S. (1999). Attitudes toward

**Indent
each**   social comparison as a function of self-esteem: Idealized appearance

following and body image. *Family & Consumer Sciences Research Journal,*
**line as you
indent a ¶** *27*, 379-405.

     Monteath, S. A., & McCabe, M. P. (1997). The influence of societal factors on

         female body image. *Journal of Social Psychology, 137*, 708-727.

     Polivy, J., & Herman, C. P. (1987). The diagnosis and treatment of abnormal

         eating. *Journal of Consulting and Clinical Psychology, 55*, 635-644.

     Pope, H. G., Bureau, B., DeCol, C., Gruber, A. J., Hudson, J. I., Jouvent, R.,

         et al. (2000). Body image perception among men in three countries.

         American Journal of Psychiatry, 157, 1297-1301.

     Rodin, J., Silberstein, L., & Striegel-Moore, R. (1984). Women and weight: A

         normative discontent. In T. B. Sonderegger (Ed.), *Nebraska symposium on*

         motivation: Psychology and gender (pp. 267-307). Lincoln: University of

         Nebraska Press.

     Rosen, J. C., & Gross, J. (1987). Prevalence of weight reducing and weight

         gaining in adolescent boys and girls. *Health Psychology, 6*, 131-147.

GUIDE TO CMS FORMATS

CMS Formats for Notes and Bibliography Entries

19 | CMS Style

The CMS (*Chicago Manual of Style*) outlines a system for references using endnotes or footnotes. These notes are less compact and less distracting than parenthetical references but allow detailed citations. Use the CMS style in academic settings in the arts and sciences, such as history, or when an instructor requests "Turabian," "Chicago," or a footnote or endnote style.

The CMS style shown here is one of two documentation systems outlined in *The Chicago Manual of Style* (15th ed., Chicago: University of Chicago Press, 2003), often simply called "Chicago." Its Web site at <http://www.chicagomanualofstyle.org/cmosfaq.html> answers many questions for writers and editors who routinely use CMS. This style is detailed for students in *A Manual for Writers of Research Papers, Theses, and Dissertations: Chicago Style for Students and Researchers,* by Kate L. Turabian and others (7th ed., Chicago: University of Chicago Press, 2007), known as "Turabian."

19a CMS endnotes and footnotes

To indicate a reference in your text, add a superscript number above the line. Number all your references consecutively. Provide the details about the source at the end of the paper (endnote) or at the bottom of the page (footnote). Because readers may skip notes, put the essentials in your text. Avoid excessive detail on points of interest to only a few readers.

A typical note supplies the author's name in regular order, title, publication information (without "Inc." and "Co."), and page reference.

TEXT   Wideman describes his childhood neighborhood as being not simply on "the wrong side of the tracks" but actually "under the tracks."[1]

NOTE   1. John Edgar Wideman, *Brothers and Keepers* (New York: Penguin Books, 1984), 39.

Though some word processors can position footnotes between the text and the bottom margin, endnotes are easy to prepare (and easy for readers to consult). Place endnotes at the end of your paper, after any appendix but before the bibliography, which alphabetically orders your sources. Begin a new page with the centered heading "Notes." For each note, indent the first line like a paragraph. Type the number on the line, followed by a period and space. Do not indent lines that follow. (See examples in 19b–c.)

CMS suggests double-spacing all parts of your text, but Turabian suggests single-spaced notes and bibliographies with an extra line between entries. Although the examples here are single-spaced to save space, we advise double-spacing for ease of reading. (Consult your instructor.)

TEXT   Another potential source of misunderstanding comes from differences in the ways orders are given by men (directly) and women (indirectly, often as requests or questions).[2]

NOTE   2. Deborah Tannen, "How to Give Orders Like a Man," *New York Times Magazine*, 18 August 1994, 46. Tannen provides a balanced, detailed discussion of the ways men and women use language in *Talking from 9 to 5* (New York: William Morrow, 1994).

19b CMS bibliography

In addition to your notes, provide readers with an alphabetical list of your sources, titled "Selected Bibliography," "Works Cited," "References," or something similar. Place this list on a new page at the end of your paper, center the title at the top, and continue the page numbering of the text. After the title, skip two lines, and begin your first entry. Do not indent the first line, but indent each subsequent line like a paragraph. Alphabetize entries by the authors' last names or by the first word of the title (excluding *A*, *An*, and *The*) if the author is unknown. (See also 19c.)

The following pairs of examples show first a note, numbered to refer to the text, and then the corresponding bibliography entry.

Books and Works Treated as Books

1. One Author

1. Bobby Bridger, *Buffalo Bill and Sitting Bull: Inventing the Wild West* (Austin: University of Texas Press, 2002), 297.

Bridger, Bobby. *Buffalo Bill and Sitting Bull: Inventing the Wild West.* Austin: University of Texas Press, 2002.

2. Two Authors

2. William H. Gerdts and Will South, *California Impressionism* (New York: Abbeville Press, 1998), 214.

Gerdts, William H., and Will South. *California Impressionism.* New York: Abbeville Press, 1998.

3. Three Authors

3. Michael Wood, Bruce Cole, and Adelheid Gealt, *Art of the Western World* (New York: Summit Books, 1989), 206-10.

Wood, Michael, Bruce Cole, and Adelheid Gealt. *Art of the Western World.* New York: Summit Books, 1989.

4. Four or More Authors

4. Anthony Slide and others, *The American Film Industry: A Historical Dictionary* (New York: Greenwood Press, 1986), 124.

Slide, Anthony, Val Almen Darez, Robert Gitt, and Susan Perez Prichard. *The American Film Industry: A Historical Dictionary.* New York: Greenwood Press, 1986.

5. No Author Given

5. *The Great Utopia* (New York: Guggenheim Museum, 1992), 661.

The Great Utopia. New York: Guggenheim Museum, 1992.

6. One Editor

6. Richard Valantasis, ed., *Religions of Late Antiquity in Practice* (Princeton: Princeton University Press, 2000), 266.

Valantasis, Richard, ed. *Religions of Late Antiquity in Practice*. Princeton: Princeton University Press, 2000.

7. Two or More Editors

7. Cris Mazza, Jeffrey DeShell, and Elisabeth Sheffield, eds., *Chick-Lit 2: No Chick Vics* (Normal, IL: Black Ice Books, 1996), 173-86.

Mazza, Cris, Jeffrey DeShell, and Elisabeth Sheffield, eds. *Chick-Lit 2: No Chick Vics*. Normal, IL: Black Ice Books, 1996.

8. Author, Editor, and Translator

8. Francis Bacon, *The New Organon*, ed. Lisa Jardine, trans. Michael Silverthorne (Cambridge: Cambridge University Press, 2000), 45.

Bacon, Francis. *The New Organon*. Edited by Lisa Jardine. Translated by Michael Silverthorne. Cambridge: Cambridge University Press, 2000.

9. Edition Following the First

9. Thomas E. Skidmore and Peter H. Smith, *Modern Latin America*, 6th ed. (New York: Oxford University Press, 2004), 243.

Skidmore, Thomas E., and Peter H. Smith. *Modern Latin America*. 6th ed. New York: Oxford University Press, 2004.

10. Reprint

10. Henri Frankfort and others, *The Intellectual Adventure of Ancient Man* (1946; repr. Chicago: University of Chicago Press, 1977), 202-4.

Frankfort, Henri, H. A. Frankfort, John A. Wilson, Thorkild Jacobsen, and William A. Irving. *The Intellectual Adventure of Ancient Man*. 1946. Reprint, Chicago: University of Chicago Press, 1977.

11. Multivolume Work

11. Sigmund Freud, *The Standard Edition of the Complete Psychological Works of Sigmund Freud*, trans. James Strachey (London: Hogarth Press, 1953), 11:180.

Freud, Sigmund. *The Standard Edition of the Complete Psychological Works of Sigmund Freud*. Translated by James Strachey. Vol. 11. London: Hogarth Press, 1953.

Articles from Periodicals and Selections from Books

12. Article in Journal Paginated by Volume

12. Lily Zubaidah Rahim, "The Road Less Traveled: Islamic Militancy in Southeast Asia," *Critical Asian Studies* 35 (2003): 224.

Rahim, Lily Zubaidah. "The Road Less Traveled: Islamic Militancy in Southeast Asia." *Critical Asian Studies* 35 (2003): 209-32.

13. Article in Journal Paginated by Issue

13. Jose Pinera, "A Chilean Model for Russia," *Foreign Affairs* 79, no. 5 (2000): 62-73.

Pinera, Jose. "A Chilean Model for Russia." *Foreign Affairs* 79, no. 5 (2000): 62-73.

14. Article in Magazine

14. Joan W. Gandy, "Portrait of Natchez," *American Legacy*, Fall 2000, 51-52.

Gandy, Joan W. "Portrait of Natchez." *American Legacy*, Fall 2000, 51-52.

15. Article in Newspaper

15. Janny Scott, "A Bull Market for Grant, A Bear Market for Lee," *New York Times*, September 30, 2000.

Scott, Janny. "A Bull Market for Grant, A Bear Market for Lee." *New York Times*, September 30, 2000.

16. Chapter in Edited Book

16. John Matviko, "Television Satire and the Presidency: The Case of *Saturday Night Live*," in *Hollywood's White House: The American Presidency in Film and History*, ed. Peter C. Rollins and John E. O'Connor (Lexington: University of Kentucky Press, 2003), 341.

Matviko, John. "Television Satire and the Presidency: The Case of *Saturday Night Live*." In *Hollywood's White House: The American Presidency in Film and History*, edited by Peter C. Rollins and John E. O'Connor, 341-60. Lexington: University of Kentucky Press, 2003.

17. Selection in Anthology

17. W. E. B. Du Bois, "The Call of Kansas," in *W. E. B. Du Bois: A Reader*, ed. David Levering Lewis (New York: Henry Holt, 1995), 113.

Du Bois, W. E. B. "The Call of Kansas." In *W. E. B. Du Bois: A Reader*, edited by David Levering Lewis, 101-21. New York: Henry Holt, 1995.

Field and Media Resources

18. Interview Unpublished

Generally treat this as a personal or informal communication, cited only in your notes.

18. LeJon Will, interview by author, May 22, 2007, transcript, Tempe, AZ.

19. Audio or Video Recording

19. *James Baldwin*, VHS, directed by Karen Thorsen (San Francisco: California Newsreel, 1990).

James Baldwin. VHS. Directed by Karen Thorsen. San Francisco: California Newsreel, 1990.

Online and Electronic Resources

20. Book: Online

20. Sharon Marcus, *Apartment Stories: City and Home in Nineteenth-Century Paris and London* (Berkeley: University of California Press, 1999), http://ark.cdlib.org/ark:13030/ft0d5n99jz/ (accessed July 1, 2007).

Marcus, Sharon. *Apartment Stories: City and Home in Nineteenth-Century Paris and London*. Berkeley: University of California Press, 1999. http://ark.cdlib.org/ark:13030/ft0d5n99jz/ (accessed July 1, 2007).

21. Older Book: Online

21. Charles Darwin, *On the Origin of Species by Means of Natural Selection, or the Preservation of Favoured Races in the Struggle for Life* (1859; Project Gutenberg, 1998), http://www.gutenberg.org/dirs/etext98/otoos11.txt (accessed July 1, 2007).

Darwin, Charles. *On the Origin of Species by Means of Natural Selection, or the Preservation of Favoured Races in the Struggle for Life*. London: Down, Bromley, Kent, 1859; Project Gutenberg, 1998. http://www.gutenberg.org/dirs/etext98/otoos11.txt (accessed July 1, 2007).

22. Journal Article: Online

22. Alfred Willis, "A Survey of Surviving Buildings of the Krotona Colony in Hollywood," *Architronic* 8, no. 1 (1999), http://architronic .saed.kent.edu/v8n1/v8n106.pdf (accessed July 2, 2007).

Willis, Alfred. "A Survey of Surviving Buildings of the Krotona Colony in Hollywood." *Architronic* 8, no. 1 (1999). http://architronic.saed .kent.edu/v8n1/v8n106.pdf (accessed July 2, 2007).

23. Magazine Article: Online

23. Alexander Barnes Dryer, "Our Liberian Legacy," *The Atlantic Online*, July 30, 2003, http://www.theatlantic.com/unbound/flashbks/ liberia.htm (accessed October 24, 2003).

Dryer, Alexander Barnes. "Our Liberian Legacy." *The Atlantic Online*, July 30, 2003. http://www.theatlantic.com/unbound/flashbks/ liberia.htm (accessed October 24, 2003).

24. Newspaper Article: Online

24. Nancy Lofholm, "Rural Giant Fading to Gray," *Denver Post*, July 1, 2007, http://www.denverpost.com/news/ci_6272010 (accessed July 1, 2007).

Lofholm, Nancy. "Rural Giant Fading to Gray." *Denver Post*, July 1, 2007. http://www.denverpost.com/news/ci_6272010 (accessed July 1, 2007).

25. Journal Article: Online Database

25. Paul Collier, "The Market for Civil War," *Foreign Policy* 136 (May-June 2003): 38-45. http://www.jstor.org/ (accessed July 1, 2007).

Collier, Paul. "The Market for Civil War." *Foreign Policy* 136 (May-June 2003): 38-45. http://www.jstor.org/ (accessed July 1, 2007).

26. Primary Material: Online Database

Cite the item in a note; if you use several items from a collection, cite it in your bibliography.

26. George A. H. Baxter, "Old Trail City," Manuscript Collection 699, box 2, Colorado Western Trails, Colorado Historical Society, http://coloradohistory.org/westerntrails/ (accessed July 16, 2007).

Colorado Western Trails, Colorado Historical Society. http://coloradohistory.org/westerntrails/ (accessed July 16, 2007).

27. Artwork or Visual: Online Database

27. John Tenniel, "Beware!" May 2, 1863. Tenniel Civil War Cartoons, ARTstor, http://0-www.artstor.org.skyline.cudenver.edu/ (accessed July 1, 2007).

Tenniel, John. Tenniel Civil War Cartoons, ARTstor. http://0-www.artstor.org.skyline.cudenver.edu/ (accessed July 1, 2007).

28. Reference Work: Online Database

Cite this only in a note; "s.v." identifies what to look under.

28. *Dictionary of American History*, s.v. "Propaganda," http://0-find.galegroup.com.skyline.cudenver.edu/gvrl/ (accessed July 12, 2007).

29. Web Site

29. Smithsonian Center for Folklife and Cultural Heritage, "2007 Smithsonian Folklife Festival: Roots of Virginia Culture," Smithsonian Institution, http://www.folklife.si.edu/festival/2007Virginia/index/htm (accessed July 2, 2007).

Smithsonian Center for Folklife and Cultural Heritage. "2007 Smithsonian Folklife Festival: Roots of Virginia Culture." Smithsonian Institution. http://www.folklife.si.edu/festival/2007Virginia/index/htm (accessed July 2, 2007).

30. Online Posting

Treat this as a personal or informal communication, cited only in your notes.

30. Justin M. Sanders, e-mail to alt.war.civil.usa, February 15, 2002, http://groups.google.com/groups?q=civil+war&hl=en&lr=&ie=UTF -8&selm=civil-war-usa/faq/part2_1013770939%40rtfm.mit.edu&rnum=1 (accessed October 21, 2003).

31. CD-ROM

31. Mark Rose, ed., "Elements of Theater," *The Norton Shakespeare Workshop CD-ROM*, CD-ROM, version 1.1 (New York: Norton Publishing, 1997).

Rose, Mark, ed. "Elements of Theater." *The Norton Shakespeare Workshop CD-ROM*. CD-ROM, version 1.1. New York: Norton Publishing, 1997.

Multiple Sources and Sources Cited in Prior Notes

32. Multiple Sources

List each source in a note separately in your bibliography.

32. See Greil Marcus, *Mystery Train: Images of America in Rock 'n Roll Music* (New York: E. P. Dutton, 1975), 119; and Susan Orlean, "All Mixed Up," New Yorker, 22 June 1992, 90.

33. Work Cited More Than Once

In your first note, provide full information. Later, provide only the author's last name, short title, and page.

33. Pinera, "Chilean," 63.

34. Wood, Cole, and Gealt, Art, 207.

If two notes in a row refer to the same source, you may use the abbreviation *Ibid.* ("in the same place") for the second note. (Specify each new page.)

35. Tarr, "'A Man,'" 183.

36. Ibid.

37. Ibid., 186.

19c CMS sample pages

Title page

Center title

DISNEY'S MAGIC MIRROR REFLECTS TRADITIONS OF OLD

Begin one-third
down the page

Kimlee Cunningham

Begin
two-thirds
down the
page

Professor Reynolds

English 201

Supply
identification
your instructor
expects

December 21, 2006

Begin on new page

↑ 1" from top ↓

↓ ½" from top

Indent ¶s ½"

1

1   Since Disney Studio's first animated feature, *Snow White and the Seven*   Double-space

Dwarfs (1937), the portrayal of female characters has changed in some obvious

White and the Seven Dwarfs with *Beauty and the Beast* (1991) and *Aladdin*

ways but has also remained the same in some key respects. Contrasting *Snow*   1" margin
on each
side

(1992) shows how the leading female characters have become more

independent and assertive. At the same time, comparing the three movies reveals the studio's continuing appeal to its audiences' sense of feminine physical beauty. Disney's contemporary portrayal of women characters shows a willingness to change with the times but also a reluctance to abandon traditional values and stereotypes.

2   It is probably an exaggeration to say that a character like Belle in *Beauty and the Beast* is a lot like a contemporary feminist, as one critic suggests.[1] However, nearly sixty years separate *Snow White and the Seven Dwarfs* from *Beauty and the Beast* and *Aladdin*. During this time of great social change, the roles of women have expanded. The shift has been from American women as housewives to American women as workers, college students, and corporate executives. By contrasting the main female character in *Snow White* with those in *Beauty* and *Aladdin*, we can see that they reflect both their own times and the social changes separating the different time periods.

Cites first source

3   In *Snow White and the Seven Dwarfs*, Snow White is portrayed as a homemaker when she and her furry and feathered companions in the forest come upon the Dwarfs' cabin. Her first reaction upon seeing the inside of the house is to begin cleaning.[2] She also becomes a mother to the Dwarfs. Before dinner, she checks their hands and sends them out to wash; later on she sends them up to bed.[3] Visually, Snow White looks like an adolescent girl with doe eyes, tiny mouth, and pure ivory skin[4] instead of looking like a woman.

Paper continues with other films

Begin on new page 2" from top   8

NOTES   Heading centered

Indent   1. Elaine Showalter, "Beauty and the Beast: Disney Meets Feminism
¹/₂" in a Liberated Love Story for the '90s," *Premiere* October 1997: 66.

2. *Snow White and the Seven Dwarfs,* VHS (1937; Walt Disney
Company, 1994).   **Numerical**
                                                                 order as
3. Ibid.   **in text**

4. Robin Allan, "Fifty Years of Snow White," *Journal of Popular
Film and Television* 24 (1988): 161.

Notes continue

Begin on new page 2" from top   9
                                                                 Page
BIBLIOGRAPHY   Heading centered   **numbers**
                                                                 continue
Aladdin. VHS. Walt Disney Company, 1993.

Indent Allan, Robin. "Fifty Years of Snow White." *Journal of Popular Film*   **1" margin**
¹/₂" for   **on each side**
lines after   *and Television* 24 (1988): 161.
first
Beauty and the Beast. VHS. Walt Disney Company, 1991.   **Alphabetical**
                                                                 order
Rosenberg, Scott. "The Genie-us of Aladdin." *San Francisco Examiner*

November 25, 1992: B2.

Showalter, Elaine. "Beauty and the Beast: Disney Meets Feminism in a

Liberated Love Story for the '90s." *Premiere* October 1997: 66.

Snow White and the Seven Dwarfs. 1937. VHS. Walt Disney Company, 1994.

Bibliography continues

20 | CSE Style

The style used by CSE (Council of Science Editors), formerly CBE (Council of Biology Editors), is a simplified international scientific style that presents two options for documentation: a name-and-year and a number system.

Use CSE style when you write in scientific or technical fields or when your instructor requests "scientific documentation" or a name-and-year or number system. CSE style tends to have more variations than other styles, mainly because different scientific fields have different requirements. Check expectations with your instructor, your readers, or the publication using the style you are following. Edit your in-text citations to follow the pattern in your model. Order the entries and arrange the details for your references in the same way, checking punctuation, capitalization, italics, and so on. For more information, see *Scientific Style and Format: The CSE Manual for Authors, Editors, and Publishers* (7th ed., Reston, VA: Council of Science Editors, 2006) or visit <http://www.councilscienceeditors.org>.

20a CSE in-text citations

With the **name-and-year method,** include the author's name and the publication date in parentheses (unless mentioned in the text).

NAMED IN PARENTHESES   Decreases in the use of lead, cadmium, and zinc have

resulted in decreased pollution (Boutron 1991).

NAMED IN TEXT   Boutron (1991) found that decreases in the use of lead,

cadmium, and zinc have decreased pollution.

Distinguish several works by the same author, all dated in a single year, by letters (*a, b, c*) after the date. Use *p* with no period before a page number.

With the **number method,** put numbers in parentheses in the text (1) or above the line[1,2]; list corresponding numbered works as references.

Decreased use of lead, cadmium, and zinc have reduced pollution (1).

20b CSE reference list

Use "References" or "Cited References" to head your list. For the name-and-year method, alphabetize sources by the last name of the main author, and then order works by the same author by date, oldest first. After the author's name, add the date and a period. For the consecutive number method, arrange sources in the same sequence in your references as in your paper. For the alphabetized number method, alphabetize the entries, number them, then use that number in your paper, noting any important author's name. The following examples illustrate the number method.

Books and Works Treated as Books

1. One Author

End the entry with the total number of pages in a book.

1. Bishop RH. Modern control systems analysis and design using MATLAB and SIMULINK. Menlo Park (CA): Addison Wesley; 1997. 251 p.

2. Two or More Authors

2. Freeman JM, Kelly MT, Freeman JB. The epilepsy diet treatment: an introduction to the ketogenic diet. New York (NY): Demo; 1994. 180 p.

3. Organization or Group Author

3. Intergovernmental Panel on Climate Change. Climate change 1995: the science of climate change. Cambridge (GB): Cambridge University Press: 1996. 572 p.

4. Editor

4. Dolphin D, editor. Biomimetic chemistry. Washington (DC): American Chemical Society; 1980. 437 p.

5. Translator

5. Jacob F. The logic of life: a history of heredity. Spillmann BE, translator. New York (NY): Pantheon Books; 1982. 348 p.

6. Conference Proceedings

6. Witt I, editor. Protein C: biochemical and medical aspects. Proceedings of the International Workshop; 1984 Jul 9-11; Titisee, Germany. Berlin (DE): De Gruyter; 1985. 195 p.

7. Report

7. Environmental Protection Agency (US) [EPA]. Guides to pollution prevention: the automotive repair industry. Washington (DC): US EPA; 1991. 46 p. Available from: EPA Office of Research and Development, Washington, DC; EPA/625/7-91/013.

Articles from Periodicals and Selections from Books

8. Article in Journal Paginated by Volume

8. Yousef YA, Yu LL. Potential contamination of groundwater from Cu, Pb, and Zn in wet detention ponds receiving highway runoff. J Environ Sci Hlth. 1992;27:1033-1044.

9. Article in Journal Paginated by Issue

9. Boutron CF. Decrease in anthropogenic lead, cadmium and zinc in Greenland snows since the late 1960's. Nature. 1991;353(6340): 153-155, 160.

10. Article with Organization or Group Author

10. Derek Sims Associates. Why and how of acoustic testing. Environ Eng. 1991;4(1):10-12.

11. Entire Issue of Journal

11. Savage A, editor. Proceedings of the workshop on the zoo-university connection: collaborative efforts in the conservation of endangered primates. Zoo Biol. 1989;1(Suppl).

12. Chapter in Edited Book or Selection in Anthology

12. Moro M. Supply and conservation efforts for nonhuman primates. In: Gengozian N, Deinhardt F, editors. Marmosets in experimental medicine. Basel (CH): S. Karger AG; 1978. p 37-40.

13. Figure from Article

13. Kanaori Y, Kawakami SI, Yairi K. Space-time distribution patterns of destructive earthquakes in the inner belt of central Japan. Eng Geol. 1991;31(3-4):209-30. Table 1; p. 216.

Online and Electronic Resources

CSE follows National Library of Medicine style for Internet items.

14. Patent from Database or Information Service

14. Russell B, inventor; Bicycle side chair apparatus. United States patent US 7,232,141. 2007 Jun 19. Available from: LexisNexis/USPatents/ AllPatents.

15. Article: Online

15. Rothe J. Heuristics versus completeness in graph coloring. Chi J Theor Comp Sci [Internet]. 2000 [cited 2007 May 9]. Available from: http://cjtcs.cs.uchicago.edu/articles/ 2000/1/ contents.html

16. Abstract: Online

16. Gruwell CA. Tracking avian flu on the Web [abstract]. Med Ref Serv Q [Internet]. 2007 [cited 2007 Jul 1]; 26(1):59-71. [1 screen]. Available from LexisNexis/Medline.

17. Book: Online

17. Darwin C. The voyage of the Beagle [Internet]. London (England): Down, Bromley, Kent; 1845 [cited 2007 Jul 1]. Available from: http://www.gutenberg.org/dirs/etext97/vbgle11.txt

20c CSE sample pages

Title page

Begin one-third down the page

Center title

Predator Occurrence at Piping Plover Nesting Sites

in Rhode Island

Center and double-space all lines

Anne S. Bloomfield

University of Rhode Island

WRT 333

Professor Robert A. Schwegler

17 April 2006

Begin on new page

Abstract

During the spring of 2006, I recorded predator occurrence based only on animal tracks on two beaches in Rhode Island. The main objective of the study was to predict the occurrence of potential predator species on piping plover (*Charadrius melodus*) nesting grounds in the area. . . .

Begin on new page   Bloomfield 1

Last name, one space, and page number

1   In Rhode Island, the threatened piping plover (*Charadrius melodus*)
prefers to breed on open beaches and sandflats.[1] Habitat destruction due to
development of beaches and predation are contributing factors to the birds'
decline.[2] For most ground-nesting bird species, the primary cause of nesting
mortality is due to egg predation.[3] I investigated the spatial distribution and
abundance of potential predators. This information, coupled with information
on plover nesting success, could be used to better manage the species. . . .

Cites sources by number

Center headings   Study Area

4   I conducted fieldwork at Moonstone Beach at Trustom Pond National
Wildlife Refuge (NWR) and East Beach at Ninigret NWR. These areas are
important seasonal nesting areas for the piping plover. Both areas are barrier
beaches with grassy dunes, bordering large coastal salt ponds. . . .

Methods

5   During my research, I based the occurrence of predators on the presence
of their tracks in the sand. At Moonstone Beach a 610 m stretch of beach was
searched. This area was searched on 24 March and 29 March for two hours
each day. The beach was marked in 30.5 m (100 ft) sections by PVC pole
markers on the foredune.

6   During each study period I recorded any factors on the beach that would
disrupt or bias data collection. This mainly included human and domestic dog
(*Canis familiaris*) tracks on the beach. I searched for tracks in each 30.5 meter
section. When a track was located, the species was recorded. . . .

Results

8   The only predatory species at Ninigret NWR was the gull (*Laridae*).
At Moonstone Beach, the spatial distribution of predators was not uniform
($P < 0.001$) with more tracks present on the section of beach extending from
pole 15 to pole 20 (Table 1). . . . Red fox (*Vulpes vulpes*) covered the
largest distance over the study area, occurring in all 20 sections during
both study periods (Figure 3). The tracks always ran in a straight path
parallel to the shore all the way across the study site and beyond.

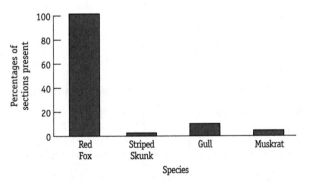

Figure 3. Occurrence of species across entire beach shows the red
fox is present all along the shore of Moonstone Beach, Rhode
Island, spring 2006

Paper continues with Discussion

References   Heading centered

1. Goldin MR, Regosin JV. Chick behavior, habitat use, and reproductive

Indent references success of piping plovers at Goosewing Beach, Rhode Island. J Field

from number Ornith. 1998:69:228-234.

2. Haig SM. Piping plover. In: Poole A, Stettenheim PS, Gill F, editors.

The birds of North America. Washington (DC): American Ornithologists'

Union; 1992. p. 1-18.

3. Skutch AF. A breeding bird census and nesting success in Central

America. Ibis. 1996:108:1-16.

4. Nol E, Brooks RJ. Effects of predator exclosures on nesting success

of killdeer. J Field Ornith. 1982:53:263-268.

5. Loegering JP, Fraser JD, Loegering LL. Ghost crab preys on piping plover

chick. Wilson Bulletin. 1995:107:768-769.

6. Wolcott DL, Wolcott TG. High mortality of piping plovers on beaches with

abundant ghost crabs: correlation, not causation. Wilson Bulletin.

1999;111:321-329.

7. Maier TJ, DeGraaf RM. Predation on Japanese quail vs. house sparrow

eggs in artificial nests: small eggs reveal small predators. Condor.

2000:102:325-332.

8. Estelle VB, Mabee TJ, Farmer AH. Effectiveness of predator exclosures for

pectoral sandpiper nests in Alaska. J Field Ornith. 1996;67:447-452.

Number
sources
(number
method)
or list alpha-
betically
(name
& year
method)

References continue

PART

4

Writing Correctly

Voices
from the Community

"All I know about grammar is its infinite power. To shift the structure of a sentence alters the meanings of that sentence, as inflexibly as the position of a camera alters the meanings of the object photographed. . . . The arrangement of the words matters, and the arrangement you want can be found in the picture in your mind."

—Joan Didion, "Why I Write"

21 Fragments

Even with a capital letter to start and a period to end, a **sentence fragment** is only part of a sentence. Words that masquerade as a sentence may irritate or mislead readers and undermine your own authority as a writer.

PARTS MISSING   The insurance company processing the claim.

            READER'S REACTION: **Something is missing. What did it do?**

EDITED   The insurance company processing the claim **sent** a check.

SERIOUS ERROR 21a Recognizing sentence fragments

Subject and verb. A **complete sentence** must contain, expressed or implied, both a **subject** (naming the doer) and a complete **verb** (naming the action or occurrence).

STRATEGY Ask questions to identify fragments and sentences.

• Test #1: Ask *who* or *what does?* Or *Who* or *what is?*

A word group that doesn't answer "Who?" or "What?" lacks a subject. If it begins with *and* or *but*, look for a nearby sentence with its subject.

FRAGMENT   And also needs a counselor.

            READER'S REACTION: **I can't tell *who* (or *what*) needs the counselor.**

EDITED   **Hope Clinic hired a nurse** and also needs a counselor.

A word group that doesn't answer "Does?" or "Is?" lacks a complete verb.

FRAGMENT   The new policy to allow overtime for extra hours.

            READER'S REACTION: **I can't tell what the policy *does* or *is*.**

EDITED   The new policy **allows** overtime for extra hours.

- Test #2: Can you turn a word group into a question that can be answered *yes* or *no*? If you can, it's a sentence.

  Caution: Begin your question with *did.* If you begin with *is, are, has,* or *have,* you may provide a missing verb.

WORD GROUPS	They signed the petition to recall the mayor. Suspecting his involvement.
QUESTIONS	Did they sign the petition to recall the mayor? [Yes.] Did suspecting his involvement? [Can't answer.]
CONCLUSION	The first word group is a sentence, but not the second.

Subordinating words. Look for a **clause** (a word group with a subject and verb) introduced by a subordinating conjunction (*although, if, because, unless;* see 31b) or a pronoun (*that, what, which, who*). If this word group is not attached to a main clause that can stand alone, it's a fragment.

STRATEGY	Hunt for a subordinating word.
FRAGMENT	Residents love the climate. <u>Which</u> is ideal for events.
EDITED	Residents love the climate **,** **which** is ideal for events.

⚠ SERIOUS ERROR 21b Editing sentence fragments

Use the following options to make your fragments complete.

STRATEGY	Attach, rewrite, add, or omit.

- Attach a fragment to a nearby sentence.

FRAGMENT	Trauma centers give prompt care to heart attack victims. <u>Because</u> **rapid treatment can minimize heart damage.**
ATTACHED	Trauma centers give prompt care to heart attack victims **because** rapid treatment can minimize heart damage.

- Rewrite to eliminate the fragment.

    FRAGMENT   **Introducing competing varieties of crabs into the same tank.** He did this in order to study aggression.

    REWRITTEN   He **introduced** competing varieties of crabs into the same tank in order to study aggression.

- Drop a subordinating word.

    FRAGMENT   <u>Although</u> **the committee contested the motion.** It still passed.

    EDITED   The committee contested the motion. It still passed.

- Supply a missing word.

    FRAGMENT   **The judge allowing adopted children to meet their natural parents.**

    EDITED   The judge **favors** allowing adopted children to meet their natural parents.

21c Using partial sentences

Especially in advertising, you'll see *deliberate* fragments used for emphasis or contrast. Use these only when readers will recognize and accept your intention. In most academic and professional writing, avoid them.

22 | Comma Splices and Fused Sentences

You may confuse or annoy readers if you inappropriately join two or more sentences using a comma (**comma splice**) or using no punctuation or connecting word at all (**fused** or **run-on sentence**).

COMMA SPLICE	CBS was founded in 1928 by William S. Paley, his uncle and his father sold him a struggling radio network.
	READER'S REACTION: At first I thought that CBS had three founders: Paley, his uncle, and his father.
EDITED	CBS was founded in 1928 by William S. Paley **;** his uncle and his father sold him a struggling radio network.
FUSED SENTENCE	The city had only one swimming pool without an admission fee the pool was in disrepair.
	READER'S REACTION: Is there only one pool, or is there only one that's free?
EDITED	The city had only one swimming pool **, but** without an admission fee, the pool was in disrepair.

22a Recognizing comma splices

Look for word groups that could stand alone but are joined by a comma.

COMMA SPLICE	The typical Navajo husband is a trustee, the wife and her children own the property.
EDITED	The typical Navajo husband is a trustee **, but** the wife and her children own the property.
	READER'S REACTION: Until you added *but*, I missed your point about the wife's status.

SERIOUS ERROR 22b Recognizing fused sentences

Though fused sentences may be any length, look for long sentences that pack in several statements without punctuation or connecting words.

FUSED SENTENCE	The scientists had trouble identifying the fossil it resembled a bird and a lizard.
EDITED	The scientists had trouble identifying the fossil **because** it resembled a bird and a lizard.
	READER'S REACTION: Adding *because* separates the two main points and clarifies the sentence.

SERIOUS ERROR

22c Editing comma splices and fused sentences

Use one of five strategies to repair comma splices or fused sentences.

1. Divide into two sentences.
   (_____. _____.)

   FUSED SENTENCE   Football does not cause the most injuries in college gymnastics is more dangerous.

   EDITED   Football does not cause the most injuries in college● **G**ymnastics is more dangerous.

2. Join with a comma plus *and, but, or, for, nor, so,* or *yet.*
   (_____, and _____.)

   FUSED SENTENCE   The clinic is understaffed it still performs well.

   EDITED   The clinic is understaffed **,** **yet** it still performs well.

3. Connect similar or equal ideas with a semicolon.
   (_____; _____.)

   COMMA SPLICE   An autopilot corrects drift, the system senses and reacts to changes in the aircraft's motion.

   EDITED   An autopilot corrects drift **;** the system senses and reacts to changes in the aircraft's motion.

4. Make one part subordinate to relate ideas.
   (Because _____, _____.)

   A subordinator (*because, though, when, unless*) or relative pronoun (*who, which, that*) can show how one idea depends on another (see 31b).

   COMMA SPLICE   Cars are so complex, mechanics may train for years.

   EDITED   **Because** cars are so complex **,** mechanics may train for years.

5. Clarify how parts relate with words and a semicolon.
   (_____; therefore, _____.)

Use words like *however* and *moreover* (conjunctive adverbs, see 31a) or *for example, consequently,* or *in contrast* <u>plus</u> a semicolon.

FUSED SENTENCE	Chickens reach market size within months the lobster takes six to eight years.
EDITED	Chickens reach market size within months **; in contrast ,** the lobster takes six to eight years.

ESL ADVICE: Similar Connecting Words

Connecting words may mean the same but need different punctuation.

Jose likes his job **, but** the hours are long.

Jose likes his job **; however ,** the hours are long.

Because introduces a clause with a subject and verb; *because of* introduces a prepositional phrase.

Because the pay is low, Anna wants a new job.

Because of the low pay, Anna wants a new job.

23 | Pronoun Reference

When you replace nouns with pronouns, you reduce repetition as you connect ideas and focus attention. Most problems occur when an **antecedent**—the word or words to which the pronoun refers—isn't clear.

AMBIGUOUS REFERENCE	In the circus, Brad's chores included leading the elephants from the cages and hosing **them** down.
	READER'S REACTION: What got hosed down? Elephants? Cages? Both?

EDITED   In the circus, Brad's chores included hosing the elephants
                down after leading **them** from **their** cages.

SERIOUS
ERROR **23a** Recognizing unclear pronoun reference

If readers say they "can't figure out what you're saying," make sure that
each pronoun refers clearly to only one possible antecedent. State the antecedent specifically, and locate it close enough to make the connection
clear.

STRATEGY   Mark a clear antecedent for each pronoun.

- Can you underline a *single, clear* antecedent?

  AMBIGUOUS   Robespierre disagreed with Danton over the path the
  REFERENCE   French Revolution should take. **He** believed that the Revo-
                 lution was endangered by internal enemies.

                 READER'S REACTION: I'm lost. Who's *he?* Robespierre or Danton?

  EDITED   Robespierre disagreed with Danton over the path the
                 French Revolution should take. **Robespierre** believed that
                 the Revolution was endangered by internal enemies.

- Can you answer, "What does [pronoun *X*] refer to?"

  IMPLIED   A hard frost damaged local citrus groves, but **it** has not
  ANTECEDENT   been determined.

                 READER'S REACTION: What does *it* mean—the frost? The damage?
                 Or something else?

  STATED   A hard frost damaged local citrus groves, but **the extent of
                 the loss** has not been determined.

SERIOUS
ERROR **23b** Editing pronoun reference

Clarify any ambiguous or vague pronoun reference.

STRATEGY **Specify or explain the pronoun.**

- Replace the pronoun with the noun to which it refers or with a synonym, or reword the sentence.

AMBIGUOUS REFERENCE	Detaching the measuring probe from the glass cylinder is a delicate job because **it** breaks easily.
	READER'S REACTION: Which is so fragile, the probe or the cylinder?
REPLACED WITH NOUN	Detaching the measuring probe from the glass cylinder is a delicate job because **the probe** breaks easily.
REWORDED	Because the measuring probe breaks easily, detaching it from the glass cylinder is a delicate job.

- After *which, this,* or *that,* specify the word to which the pronoun refers.

VAGUE REFERENCE	Redfish have suffered from oil pollution and the destruction of their swamp habitat. **This** has reduced the redfish population.
	READER'S REACTION: Does *this* refer to the destruction of habitat, the pollution, or both?
SPECIFIED	Redfish have suffered from oil pollution and the destruction of their swamp habitat. **This combination** has reduced the redfish population.

Sometimes a pronoun doesn't have to be replaced, just moved—especially to place *who, which,* and *that* right after their antecedents.

CONFUSING	After our dog died, I found an old ball behind **a bush that he loved to chase.**
EDITED	After our dog died, I found behind a bush an **old ball that he loved to chase.**

Especially for many academic readers, a possessive noun used as an antecedent will appear to be an error.

> **STRATEGY** **Eliminate the possessive, and rewrite.**
>
> **INAPPROPRIATE** In Faulkner's *The Sound and the Fury*, **he** begins from the point of view of a mentally retarded person.
>
> **EDITED** In *The Sound and the Fury*, **Faulkner** begins from the point of view of a mentally retarded person.

24 | Agreement

You give readers mixed signals if you don't coordinate sentence parts grammatically. Readers expect to see how ideas in a sentence relate to each other by showing **agreement** in number, person, and gender.

INCONSISTENT The city council and the mayor is known for her skillful responses to civic debate.

> **READER'S REACTION: This sentence opens with two things—the city council and the mayor—but *is* and *her* seem to switch to only the mayor.**

EDITED The city council and the mayor **are** known for **their** skillful responses to civic debate.

SERIOUS ERROR · 24a Recognizing agreement

A subject and verb in a sentence should agree in number and person. A pronoun (*I, you, she*) should agree with its **antecedent,** the noun or other pronoun to which it refers, in number, person, and gender.

AGREEMENT: NUMBER, PERSON, GENDER

- **Number** shows singular (one) or plural (two or more) items.

  This **community** <u>needs</u> <u>its</u> recreation center.

  These **communities** <u>need</u> to share <u>their</u> facilities.

- **Person** indicates the speaker or subject spoken to or about.

FIRST PERSON (SPEAKER)	I, we
SECOND PERSON (SPOKEN TO)	You, you
THIRD PERSON (SPOKEN ABOUT)	He, she, it, they

- **Gender** refers to masculine (*he, him*), feminine (*she, her*), or neuter (*it*) qualities attributed to a noun or pronoun.

SERIOUS
ERROR

24b Editing subject-verb agreement

Subjects and verbs should match, both singular or both plural.

STRATEGY Check the *-s* and *-es* endings.

Add *-s* or *-es* to make nouns plural but present tense verbs singular.

SINGULAR	The dam prevent**s** flooding. [third person]
PLURAL	The dam**s** prevent flooding.

Exceptions

- **Nouns with irregular plurals** (*person/people, child/children*) or with the same form for singular and plural (*moose/moose*)
- **Verbs with irregular forms,** including *be* and *have*

More complicated sentences may lead you to use the wrong verb form.

STRATEGY Find the *real* subject, and match the verb.

- Mark the subject (not nouns in other word groups). Decide whether it's singular or plural. Edit the verb (or change the subject) to agree.

DRAFT	The use of new testing **techniques** have increased.
REAL SUBJECT	The <u>use</u> of new testing **techniques** <u>have increased</u>.
EDITED	The **use** of new testing techniques **has increased.**

- Imagine the core sentence without any intervening expressions. Make the central noun and verb agree.

DRAFT	A regular tune-up, along with frequent oil changes, pro-long the life of your car.
	IMAGINE: A regular tune-up, ~~along with frequent oil changes,~~ <u>prolong</u> the life of your car.
EDITED	A regular <u>tune-up</u>, along with frequent oil changes, <u>prolongs</u> the life of your car.

ESL ADVICE: Separated Subjects and Verbs

PHRASE   A <u>person</u> **with sensitive eyes** <u>has</u> to wear sunglasses.

CLAUSE   A <u>person</u> **whose eyes are sensitive** <u>has</u> to wear sunglasses.

When the subject is the same in both clauses, the verbs must agree.

SAME SUBJECT   A <u>person</u> who <u>wants</u> to protect her eyes <u>wears</u> sunglasses.

Deciding whether some nouns are singular or plural can be tricky.

STRATEGY   **Use a pronoun to test your verb choice.**

Decide which pronoun accurately represents a complicated subject: *he, she,* or *it* (singular) or *they* (plural). Read your sentence aloud using this replacement pronoun; edit the verb to agree.

DRAFT	The **news** about the job market [sounds? sound?] good.
	PRONOUN TEST: I could say "it" for "The news": "It sounds."
EDITED	The **news** about the job market **sounds** good.

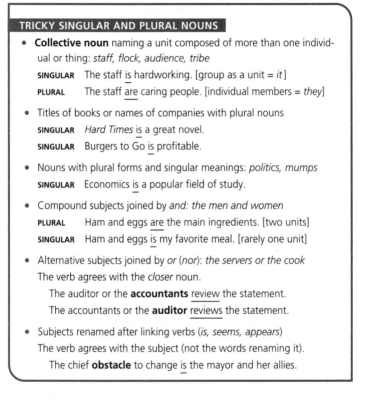

TRICKY SINGULAR AND PLURAL NOUNS

- **Collective noun** naming a unit composed of more than one individual or thing: *staff, flock, audience, tribe*

  SINGULAR The staff is hardworking. [group as a unit = *it*]

  PLURAL The staff are caring people. [individual members = *they*]

- Titles of books or names of companies with plural nouns

  SINGULAR *Hard Times* is a great novel.

  SINGULAR Burgers to Go is profitable.

- Nouns with plural forms and singular meanings: *politics, mumps*

  SINGULAR Economics is a popular field of study.

- Compound subjects joined by *and: the men and women*

  PLURAL Ham and eggs are the main ingredients. [two units]

  SINGULAR Ham and eggs is my favorite meal. [rarely one unit]

- Alternative subjects joined by *or* (*nor*): *the servers or the cook*

  The verb agrees with the *closer* noun.

  The auditor or the **accountants** review the statement.

  The accountants or the **auditor** reviews the statement.

- Subjects renamed after linking verbs (*is, seems, appears*)

  The verb agrees with the subject (not the words renaming it).

  The chief **obstacle** to change is the mayor and her allies.

Indefinite pronouns do not refer to specific ideas, people, or things. Most (*anyone, each*) require singular verbs, but a few (*both, few*) need plural verbs. Some (*all, most, some*) may be singular (for something that cannot be counted) or plural (for two or more items that can be counted).

SINGULAR **All** of the food **is** gone.

food = food in general (not countable)

PLURAL **All** of the supplies **are** gone.
supplies = many kinds (countable)

ESL ADVICE: Quantifiers

Quantifiers (*each, one, many*) show the amount or quantity of a noun.

EXPRESSIONS FOLLOWED BY PLURAL NOUN + SINGULAR VERB
Each of/Every one of/One of/None of   the **students** lives on campus.

EXPRESSIONS FOLLOWED BY PLURAL NOUN + PLURAL VERB
Several of/Many of/Both of   the **students** live off campus.

EXPRESSIONS FOLLOWED BY A SINGULAR OR A PLURAL VERB

                                noncount noun + singular verb
Some of/Most of/All of/A lot of   the **produce** is fresh.

                                plural noun + plural verb
Some of/Most of/All of/A lot of   the **vegetables** are fresh.

MUCH AND *MOST* (WITHOUT *OF*)

NONCOUNT NOUN   **Much traffic** occurs during rush hour.
PLURAL NOUN   **Most Americans** live in or near cities.

TRICKY SINGULAR AND PLURAL PRONOUNS

- *Who, which*, and *that* as subjects of clauses

  Match the verb and the word to which the pronoun refers.

  He likes a film that builds suspense but novels that show character.

- *Each* or *every* before a compound subject

  SINGULAR   Each clerk and manager checks the log.

- *Each* and *every* after a compound subject

  PLURAL   The clerks and managers each check the log.

24c Editing pronoun-antecedent agreement

Work with either the pronoun or its **antecedent,** the word to which it refers. Edit to bring the other into agreement.

STRATEGY Mark the specific word to which a pronoun refers.

INCONSISTENT	**Each** of the samples travels in their own case.
CLEAR	**Each** of the samples travels in its own case.

When indefinite pronouns (see pp. 157–58) are singular, so are other pronouns that refer to them.

Somebody on the team left her racket on the court.

Each of the men has his own equipment.

To avoid sexist language, use plural pronouns and antecedents.

SEXIST	**Everybody** used charts in **his** sales **talk.**
SPOKEN	**Everybody** used charts in **their** sales **talks.**
WRITTEN	**All presenters** used charts in **their** sales **talks.**

ESL ADVICE: *This, That, These, Those*

To modify nouns, *this* and *that* are singular; *these* and *those* are plural.

INCONSISTENT	This crystals make snowflakes.
PLURAL	**These crystals** make snowflakes.
INCONSISTENT	Those experiment takes two days.
SINGULAR	**That experiment** takes two days.

25 | Correct Forms

If you misuse word forms, readers may doubt your ability as a writer and pay more attention to the error than to your point.

DRAFT   By Friday, him and me will submit the report.

READER'S REACTION: *Him and me* **sounds uneducated. Who hired this person?**

EDITED   By Friday, **he and I** will submit the report.

25a Recognizing and editing verb forms

Verbs vary in **tense** as they show past, present, and future time.

Past tense *-ed* ending for regular verbs.   Be sure to write this ending even if you don't hear it pronounced before a *-d* or *-t* sound.

DRAFT   The company **use** to provide dental benefits.

EDITED   The company **used** to provide dental benefits.

Past tense irregular verbs.   Irregular verbs form the past tense in some way other than adding *-ed* (*run/ran*). (For examples, see p. 162.)

DRAFT   The movie characters **sweared** constantly.

EDITED   The movie characters **swore** constantly.

Verb forms in complex tenses.   Complex tenses (see pp. 162–63) have a helping verb and then a main verb. The **helping verb** is a form of *be, do,* or *have* or a verb such as *will* or *would*. The main verb is a **participle, past** (*-ed, -en,* or irregular form) or **present** (*-ing* form).

-ING FORM	He <u>was</u> **loading** the delivery van. (present participle)
REGULAR VERB	Mike <u>has</u> **analyzed** the problem. (past participle)
IRREGULAR VERB	Lynn <u>has</u> **brought** the equipment. (past participle)

ESL ADVICE: Common Helping Verbs

Be: *am, is, are, was, were, be, being, been*
Have: *have, has, had*
Do: *do, does, did*
Modals: *could, should, would, ought to, can, may, might, must, shall, will*

Helping verbs in progressive tenses. These forms show an action in progress using an *-ing* main verb: *is turning, was turning, will be turning* (see p. 163). Write all parts of the verb even if your spoken dialect omits them.

WORD OMITTED	The interview **starting** now.
EDITED	The interview **is starting** now.
WRONG FORM	The workers **was running** for the door.
EDITED	The workers **were running** for the door.

Past participles in perfect tenses. These tenses combine a helping verb with a past participle (*-ed*, *-en*, or irregular) to show the order of events (see pp. 162–63). Don't substitute the simple past for the past participle.

MISTAKEN PAST	Pete **had rode** for a year before his injury.
EDITED	Pete **had ridden** for a year before his injury.

VERB FORMS

PRINCIPAL PARTS OF VERBS

	BASE FORM	PAST	PRESENT PARTICIPLE	PAST PARTICIPLE
REGULAR	live	lived	living	lived
IRREGULAR	eat	ate	eating	eaten
	run	ran	running	run

SOME COMMON IRREGULAR VERB FORMS

PRESENT	PAST	PAST PARTICIPLE
arise	arose	arisen
be	was/were	been
bring	brought	brought
come	came	come
go	went	gone
ride	rode	ridden
see	saw	seen
take	took	taken
write	wrote	written

See also the Glossary of Usage and Terms.

VERB TENSES IN THE ACTIVE VOICE

Present: action taking place now, including habits and facts

I/you/we/they	examine/begin
he/she/it	examines/begins

Past: action that has already taken place at an earlier time

I/you/he/she/it/we/they	examined/began

Future: action that will take place at an upcoming time

I/you/he/she/it/we/they	will examine/begin

Present Perfect: action that has recurred or continued

I/you/we/they	have examined/begun
he/she/it	has examined/begun

Past Perfect: action that had already taken place
I/you/he/she/it/we/they   had examined/begun

Future Perfect: action that will have taken place
I/you/he/she/it/we/they   will have examined/begun

Present Progressive: action that is in progress now, at this moment
I   am examining/beginning
you/we/they   are examining/beginning
he/she/it   is examining/beginning

Past Progressive: action that was in progress earlier
I/he/she/it   was examining/beginning
you/we/they   were examining/beginning

Future Progressive: action that will be in progress
I/you/he/she/it/we/they   will be examining/beginning

Present Perfect Progressive: action in progress up to now
I/you/we/they   have been examining/beginning
he/she/it   has been examining/beginning

Past Perfect Progressive: action already in progress
I/you/he/she/it/we/they   had been examining/beginning

Future Perfect Progressive: action that will have been in progress
I/you/he/she/it/we/they   will have been examining/beginning

Mood. Sentences can be classified by **mood,** the form of the verb that reflects the writer's or speaker's attitude. **Indicative** statements are intended as truthful or factual: Motorcycle helmets *have reduced* injuries. **Imperative** statements acts as commands: *Get* a helmet. **Subjunctive** statements express uncertainty—a supposition, prediction, possibility, desire, or wish.

If you **were** to crash, the helmet would protect your head.

Jim's insurance requires that he **wear** a helmet.

The subjunctive appears in formal writing, often in **conditional statements** beginning with *if* and in *that* clauses with verbs such as *ask* or *request*. With *that*, use the basic present form (*wear, be*), even with the third person singular. With *if*, use the basic present, the past (*wore, were* not *was*), or the past perfect (*had worn* not *would have worn, had been*).

ESL ADVICE: Conditional Statements

Conditional statements depend on a condition or are imagined. Each type has an *if* clause and a result clause that combine different verb tenses.

Type I: True in the present

- Generally true in the present as a habit or as a fact

  if + subject + <u>present tense</u>   **subject + <u>present tense</u>**
  If **I** <u>drive</u> to school every day,   **I** <u>get</u> to class on time.

- True in the future as a one-time event

  if + subject + <u>present tense</u>   **subject + <u>future tense</u>**
  If **I** <u>drive</u> to school today,   **I** <u>will get</u> to class on time.

- Possibly true in the future as a one-time event

  if + subject + <u>present tense</u>   **subject + <u>modal + base form verb</u>**
  If **I** <u>drive</u> to school today,   **I** <u>may get</u> to class on time.

Type II: Untrue or contrary to fact in the present

  if + subject + <u>past tense</u>   **subject + <u>*would/could/might*</u> + base form verb**
  If **I** <u>drove</u> to school,   **I** <u>would arrive</u> on time.

For Type II, the form of *be* in the *if* clause is always *were*.

Type III: Untrue or contrary to fact in the past

                         subject + <u>*would/could/might*</u> +
  if + subject + <u>past perfect tense</u>   **<u>*have*</u> + past participle**
  If **I** <u>had driven</u> to school,   **I** <u>would not have been</u> late.

Voice. Verbs in the **active voice** appear in sentences in which the doer (or agent) of an action is the subject of the sentence.

	DOER (SUBJECT)	ACTION (VERB)	GOAL (OBJECT)
ACTIVE	The car	**hit**	the lamppost.
ACTIVE	Dana	**distributed**	the flyers.

A verb in the **passive voice** adds a form of *be* as a helping verb to the past participle form. The subject (or doer) may appear as an object after the word *by* in an optional prepositional phrase. (See 26b.)

	GOAL (SUBJECT)	ACTION (VERB)	[DOER: PREPOSITIONAL PHRASE]
PASSIVE	The lamppost	**was hit**	[by the car].
PASSIVE	The flyers	**were distributed**	[by Dana].

Lie, lay, sit, set. These forms are confusing for many writers.

VERB	PRESENT	PAST	PAST PARTICIPLE
lie (oneself)	lie	lay	lain
lay (an object)	lay	laid	laid
sit (oneself)	sit	sat	sat
set (an object)	set	set	set

DRAFT	I **laid** down for yoga. I **have laid** down every class.
EDITED	I **lay** down for yoga. I **have lain** down every class.

DRAFT	Erica and Steve **sat** the projector on the table.
EDITED	Erica and Steve **set** the projector on the table.

25b Editing for clear tense sequence

Readers expect you to use one tense or to follow a logical sequence.

STRATEGY Change tense to relate events in time.

LOGICAL   People **forget** that four candidates **ran** in 1948.

| LOGICAL | The accountant **destroyed** the file because **no one had asked** him to save it. |
| LOGICAL | No one **had recognized** that food from cans sealed with lead solder **is** poisonous. |

25c Recognizing pronoun forms

Pronouns change form to fit their roles in a sentence.

SUBJECT	I, you, he, she, it; we, you, they
	I ran out of leaflets, but **he** had plenty.
OBJECT	me, you, him, her, it; us, you, them
	Jamie gave **me** some extras for **them.**
POSSESSIVE	my, mine, your, yours, his, her, hers, its; our, ours, your, yours, their, theirs (but not *it's* = *it is*; see 36d)
	Our client chose **my** leaflet design, not **hers.**

To rename a subject after *be* (*is, are, was, were*), use the subjective form.

   subject   subject complement
The people assigned the report <u>were</u> **Trinh and I.**

STRATEGY Test for pronouns that rename the subject.

Reverse the sentence to make the pronoun the subject.

DRAFT	**The last art majors** to get jobs were Becky and **me.**
REVERSED	Becky and **me** were the last art majors to get jobs.
REVERSE TEST	**Me** was the last art major. [doesn't fit]
EDITED	The last art majors to get jobs were Becky and **I.**

25d Editing pronoun forms

Compound subjects and objects. Use the same form for a pronoun in a compound that you would use if it were by itself.

| STRATEGY | **Try focus-imagine-choose.** |

- **Focus** on the questionable pronoun.

| DRAFT | Anna and **me** will develop the video. |
| | FOCUS: *I* or *me?* |

- **Imagine** each choice for the pronoun.

  Me will develop the video. (no)   **I** will develop the video. (yes)

- **Choose** the correct form for the compound.

| EDITED | Anna and **I** will develop the video. |

Appositives. When you rename a preceding noun or pronoun in an **appositive,** match the pronoun to the form of the word being renamed.

| STRATEGY | **Test possible replacements.** |

DRAFT	The two panelists, **her** and **me,** answered questions.
REPLACEMENT	**Her** and **me** answered questions. (no)
REPLACEMENT	**She** and **I** answered questions. (yes)
EDITED	The two panelists, **she and I,** answered questions.

Comparisons with *than* or *as*. When you end a comparison with a pronoun, choose the form based on the information left out.

| SUBJECT | I gave her sister more help than **she** [did]. |
| OBJECT | I gave her sister more help than [I gave] **her.** |

***Who* and *whom*.** Choose *who* and *whoever* as subjects; choose *whom* and *whomever* as objects. When the pronoun is in a clause, make your choice based on its role within the clause, not the sentence as a whole.

SUBJECT	**Who** has the reader's sympathy, Huck or Jim?
OBJECT	Give this task to **whomever you trust.**
SUBJECT	The fine must be paid by **whoever holds the deed.**

25e Recognizing adjectives and adverbs

Adjectives and adverbs **modify** other words, adding to, qualifying, limiting, or extending their meaning.

FEATURES OF ADJECTIVES AND ADVERBS

ADJECTIVES

- Modify nouns and pronouns
- Answer "How many?" "What kind?" "Which one (or ones)?" "What size, color, or shape?"
- Include words such as *blue, complicated*, and *good*
- Include words created by adding endings such as *-able, -ical, -less, -ful*, and *-ous* to nouns or verbs (*sociological, seamless, nervous*)

ADVERBS

- Modify verbs, adjectives, and other adverbs
- Modify phrases (*almost* over the hill), clauses (*soon after* I added the eggs), and sentences (*Remarkably*, the mechanism was unharmed.)
- Answer "When?" "Where?" "How?" "How often?" "Which direction?" "What degree?"
- Include mostly words ending in *-ly* (*quickly*) but also some words that do not end in *-ly* (*fast, very, well, quite, late*)

SERIOUS ERROR

25f Editing adjectives and adverbs

Because not all adverbs end in *-ly* and some adjectives do (*friendly*), the *-ly* ending won't always help you pick the form. If you can't tell which to use, ask the questions in the box above or point to the word modified.

DRAFT   Write **careful** so the directions are clear.
               QUESTION: **Write *how?* It answers an adverb question.**

EDITED   Write **carefully** so the directions are clear.

TRICKY ADJECTIVES AND ADVERBS

BAD/BADLY

Use *bad* (adjective) with linking
verbs (*is, seems, appears*).
Use *badly* (adverb) with action
verbs.

I feel **bad** that our group
argues so much.
The new breathing apparatus
works **badly.**

GOOD/WELL

Use *good* (adjective) with linking
verbs (*is, seems*).
Use *well* (adverb) with action verbs
unless it refers to health.

The chef's new garlic dressing
tastes **good.**
The new pump works **well.**
Nan looks **well.** [health]

REAL/REALLY

Use *really* (adverb), not *real*, to
modify an adjective or adverb.

Lu Ming is **really** efficient.
Lu Ming works **really** efficiently.

Modifiers with linking verbs. Verbs such as *look, feel,* and *prove* can
show both states of being (**linking verbs**) and activities (**action verbs**).
Use an adjective for a state of being and an adverb for an activity.

ADJECTIVE (BEING)	The metal cover over the motor turned **hot.**
ADVERB (ACTION)	The large wheel turned **quickly.**
ADJECTIVE	The movement grew **rapid.** [The motion became quick.]
ADVERB	The movement grew **rapidly.** [The group spread its ideas.]

SERIOUS ERROR **Double negatives.** Readers are likely to feel that two negatives (*no, none, not, never, hardly, scarcely, don't*) cancel each other out.

DRAFT	The nurses **can't hardly** manage the emergencies.
	READER'S REACTION: This sounds like conversation, not a report.
EDITED	The nurses **can hardly** manage the emergencies.

ESL ADVICE: Articles and Nouns

The **indefinite articles** are *a* and *an*; the **definite article** is *the*.

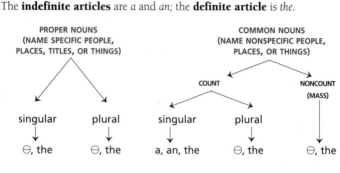

PROPER NOUNS
(NAME SPECIFIC PEOPLE,
PLACES, TITLES, OR THINGS)

COMMON NOUNS
(NAME NONSPECIFIC PEOPLE,
PLACES, OR THINGS)

COUNT

NONCOUNT
(MASS)

singular   plural   singular   plural

⊖, the   ⊖, the   a, an, the   ⊖, the   ⊖, the

⊖ = no article

Proper nouns usually use no article (singular) and *the* (plural).

SINGULAR   Rosa Parks helped initiate the civil rights movement.

PLURAL   **The** Everglades have abundant wildlife.

Count nouns name items that can be counted: *two chairs, a hundred beans*.

Singular count nouns cannot stand alone. Use *a* or *an* when you are not referring to any specific person or thing.

I need **a** car to go to work. [unknown, nonspecific, or any car]

Use *the* when you are referring to an exact, known person or thing.

I need **the** car to go to work. [specific, known car]

Plural count nouns use no article (if general) or *the* (if specific).

GENERALIZATION   Books are the best teachers.

SPECIFIC   **The** books on his desk are due Monday.

Noncount (mass) nouns name material or abstractions that cannot be counted: *flour, water, steel*. They never use *a* or *an* but may stand alone (if general) or use *the* (if specific).

GENERAL   <u>Laughter</u> is good medicine.

SPECIFIC   **The** <u>laughter</u> of children is good medicine.

Use *the* when a noun is followed by a modifier, such as an adjective clause or prepositional phrase, that makes the noun specific.

PLURAL COUNT   **The** <u>airline tickets</u> that you bought are at half price.

NONCOUNT   **The** <u>information</u> on the flight board has changed.

25g Recognizing and editing comparisons

For most modifiers, choose the form based on how many things you compare, **positive** (no others), **comparative** (two things; *-er* or *more*), **superlative** (three or more things; *-est* or *most*).

POSITIVE   The liquid flowed **quickly** from the **large** beaker.

COMPARATIVE   The liquid flowed **more quickly** from the **larger** beaker.

SUPERLATIVE   The liquid flowed **most quickly** from the **largest** beaker.

Most readers won't accept double comparative forms.

DRAFT   Jorge is the **most agilest** athlete.

EDITED   Jorge is the **most agile** athlete.

Illogical comparisons.   Some adjectives and adverbs, such as *unique, impossible, pregnant,* and *dead,* can't logically take comparative forms.

ILLOGICAL   Gottlieb's *Nightscape* is **most unique.**

                 READER'S REACTION: **How can this painting be *more* or *most* if it's *unique*—the only one?**

LOGICAL   Gottlieb's *Nightscape* is **unique.**

ESL ADVICE: Prepositions

Time: Use *at* for a specific time. Use *on* for days and dates. Use *in* for non-specific times during a day, month, season, or year. Use *for* with an amount of time (hours, days, years) and *since* with a specific time.

> Brandon was born **at** 11:11 a.m. **on** *a* Monday **in** 1996.

> The office has been open **for** two hours **since** 9 a.m.

Place: Use *at* for specific addresses, *on* for street names, and *in* for areas.

> She lives **on** Town Avenue but works **at** 99 Low Street **in** Dayton.

Use *to* for most expressions of going to a place.

> I am going **to** work.   I am going **to** the library.

In some cases, use no preposition: I am going home.

Both: Arrange prepositional phrases in this order: place, then time.

> The runners will start **in the park** <u>on Saturday</u>

Prepositions with nouns, verbs, and adjectives: Nouns, verbs, and adjectives may appear with certain prepositions.

NOUN + PREPOSITION	He has an <u>understanding</u> **of** global politics.
VERB + PREPOSITION	Managers <u>worry</u> **about** many things.

Voices
from the Community

"The difference between the almost right word and the right word is really a large matter—it's the difference between the lightning bug and the lightning."

—Mark Twain, from a letter
to George Bainton

26 | Clear Sentences

Readers in all communities value clear writing that's easy to read even if it presents complex ideas and reasoning.

INDIRECT OR EVASIVE
It is suggested that employee work cooperation encouragement be used for product quality improvement.

READER'S REACTION: Who is suggesting this? What is "employee work cooperation encouragement"?

CLEAR
We will try to improve our products by encouraging employees to work cooperatively.

26a Recognizing unclear sentences

Clear sentences answer "Who does what (to whom)?" When a sentence doesn't readily do so, make its subject and verb easy for readers to identify.

UNCLEAR
One suggestion offered by physicians is that there is a need to be especially observant of a baby after the injection.

READER'S REACTION: Who's doing the observing?

CLEAR
Physicians suggest that parents watch babies carefully after the injection.

26b Editing for clear sentences

Readers need to identify subjects (who) and verbs (did what) easily.

STRATEGY Find your significant subject.

- Ask "Who (or what) am I talking about here?"
- Ask "Is this what I want to emphasize?"

UNFOCUSED	You run the greatest risk if you expose yourself to tanning machines as well as the sun because both can damage the skin.
	READER'S REACTION: **Isn't the point the danger posed by sunbathing and tanning? Why are they both buried in the middle?**
EDITED	Either **the sun or a tanning machine** can damage the skin, and exposure to **both** causes the greatest risk.

Weak nouns. When you create a noun (*completion, happiness*) from another kind of word such as a verb (*complete*) or an adjective (*happy*), you **nominalize** that word. Replace each weak nominalization with a clear and significant subject (or object). Name the action (did what?) in the verb.

Weak verbs. Forms of the verb *be* (*is, are, was, were*) show being, not action, and may create dull sentences. Instead, energize your verbs.

- Use more forceful verbs in place of forms of *be*.

WEAK	The program **is a money saver.**
STRONGER	The program **saves money.**

- Turn nouns into verbs to replace general verbs (*give, have, get, make*).

WEAK	We **have done** a <u>study</u> of the project and **will provide** <u>funding</u> for it.
STRONGER	We **have studied** the project and **will fund** it.

- Drop indirect "there is," "there are," and "it is" patterns.

DRAFT	**There is** a need for more classrooms at Kenny School.
EDITED	Kenny School needs more classrooms.

ESL Advice: *There* and *It* as Subjects

There and *it* as subjects can refer to a thing or place (as in *The car is there* or *What did it* [the book, for example] *say?*). *There* also may introduce new material, and *it* may refer to weather, time, or distance.

DRAFT	Although there was snowing, it still was dancing after dinner.
EDITED	Although **it** was snowing, **there** still was dancing after dinner.

Unnecessary passive voice. Passive voice focuses on action, not agent, turning the doer into the receiver of action. Active voice puts the doer into the first, or subject, position (see 25a).

PASSIVE   **The people** affected by the toxin were contacted by **the Centers for Disease Control.**

ACTIVE   **The Centers for Disease Control** contacted the people affected by the toxin.

Separated subject and verb. Too much distance between a subject and a verb can make a sentence difficult to read.

CONFUSING   The <u>veterinary association</u>, **in response to the costly guidelines for disposal of medical waste,** <u>has created</u> a low-cost loan program for its members.

EDITED   **In response to the costly guidelines for disposal of medical waste,** the <u>veterinary association</u> <u>has created</u> a low-cost loan program for its members.

27 | Mixed Structures

When you're reading, you can't ask the writer to explain a confusing shift of topic or a grammatical pattern.

TOPIC SHIFT   One **skill** I envy is **a person** who can meet deadlines.
              READER'S REACTION: **Does this mean a *skill* is a *person*?**

EDITED   One **skill** I envy is **the ability** to meet deadlines.

27a Recognizing mixed and incomplete sentences

In most sentences, the subject announces a topic, and the **predicate** (the verb and words that complete it) comments on or renames the topic. With a **topic shift** (**faulty predication**), the second part of the sentence comments on or names a topic different from the one announced. With a **mixed grammatical pattern,** the sentence shifts between patterns.

STRATEGY **Look for topic and comment.**

- Read your sentences aloud for *meaning,* especially how the topic (subject) and comment (predicate) relate.
- Ask "Who does what?" or "What is it?" If the answer is illogical, edit.
- Ask "What's the topic? How does the rest comment on or rename it?"
- Ask "Does the sentence clearly tell who does what to whom?"

TOPIC SHIFT   In this factory, **flaws** in the product noticed by any worker **can stop** the assembly line.
READER'S REACTION: **Who does what? Flaws can't stop the line.**

EDITED   In this factory, **any worker** who notices flaws in the product **can stop** the assembly line.

27b Editing mixed and incomplete sentences

State your topic; then imagine what readers will expect next.

- Keep the topics on each side of *be* equivalent; make sure the second part of the sentence renames the topic in the first part.

TOPIC SHIFT   **Irradiation** is **food** that is preserved by radiation.

EDITED   **Irradiation** is a **process** used to preserve food.

- Drop *is when* and *is where;* they create an imbalance on both sides of *be.*

  NOT BALANCED **Blocking** is **when** a network schedules a less popular program between two popular ones.

  EDITED **Blocking** is the **practice** of scheduling a less popular program between two popular ones.

- Rewrite to eliminate *the reason . . . is because.*

  Readers expect the subject (topic) to be renamed after *is.* When *because* appears there instead, they find the sentence illogical.

  DRAFT The **reason** he took up skating **is because** he wanted winter exercise.

  EDITED The reason he took up skating **is that** he wanted winter exercise. [Change *because* to *that.*]

  EDITED He took up skating **because** he wanted winter exercise. [Drop *the reason . . . is.*]

Inconsistent sentence patterns. If you mistake words between the subject and verb for the sentence topic, you may mix up different patterns.

> **STRATEGY** Make the topic for subject and verb the same.
>
> **TOPIC SHIFT** Programming **decisions** by TV executives <u>consider</u> the need for audience share.
>
> **READER'S REACTION:** How can decisions think?
>
> **EDITED** When **making** programming decisions, **TV executives** <u>consider</u> the need for audience share.

Incomplete and illogical comparisons. You can sometimes simplify by omitting repeated elements that readers can supply. But if you cut essentials, you may create an **incomplete comparison,** lacking words needed for clarity, or an **illogical comparison,** comparing things that aren't comparable.

STRATEGY	**Add missing words or a possessive to compare logically.**
ILLOGICAL	The fat content in even a small hamburger is more than a skinless chicken breast.
	READER'S REACTION: The fat is more than the chicken breast?
EDITED	The fat content in even a small hamburger is more than **that in** a skinless chicken breast.
EDITED	Even a small **hamburger's** fat content is more than a skinless chicken **breast's.**

28 | Dangling and Misplaced Modifiers

Because a **modifier** qualifies, adds to, or limits the meaning of another word or word group, it needs to be positioned logically. Otherwise, readers may find a sentence vague, illogical, or even humorous.

MISPLACED MODIFIER	The wife believes she sees a living figure behind the wallpaper in the story by Charlotte Perkins Gilman, which adds to her sense of entrapment.
	READER'S REACTION: How could a story add to a feeling of entrapment?
MODIFIER MOVED	The wife **in the story by Charlotte Perkins Gilman** believes she sees a living figure behind the wallpaper, which adds to her sense of entrapment.

SERIOUS ERROR

28a Recognizing misplaced modifiers

To recognize a **misplaced modifier,** look for a word or word group that is not positioned closely enough to the word or words it modifies—its **headword**—and instead appears to modify some other word.

MISPLACED   The caterer served food to the clients standing around the
                room on flimsy paper plates.
                READER'S REACTION: **Surely clients didn't stand on plates!**

MOVED   The caterer served food **on flimsy paper plates** to the clients
                standing around the room.

Dangling modifier. Look for a sentence that begins with a modifier but doesn't name what's modified. Readers will think the modifier refers to the subject of the sentence that follows. If it doesn't, the modifier dangles.

DANGLING   **Looking** for a way to reduce complaints from nonsmok-
                ers, **a ventilation fan** was installed.
                READER'S REACTION: **How could a fan look for anything?**

SUBJECT ADDED   **Looking** for a way to reduce complaints from nonsmokers,
                the company installed a ventilation fan.

Squinting modifier. Look for a word that appears to modify both the words before and after. These are often misplaced **limiting modifiers**, words like *only, almost, hardly, just, scarcely,* and *even* that can move around in a sentence, generally changing meaning as they do.

SQUINTING   Students who binge drink **often** skip classes.
                READER'S REACTION: **Do they *binge drink often* or *often skip*?**

EDITED   Students who **often** binge drink may skip classes.

Split infinitives. Some readers find words placed between the parts of an infinitive (*to* plus a verb) irritating. Balance this risk against the directness a split infinitive sometimes offers.

IRRITATING?   The dancers moved **to very rapidly align** themselves.

EDITED   The dancers moved **very rapidly to align** themselves.

SERIOUS ERROR ⚠ 28b Editing misplaced modifiers

Make sure modifiers clearly relate to the words they qualify.

> **STRATEGY**   **Position and connect modifiers logically.**

- Place *who, which,* or *that* close to its headword.

    MISPLACED   The inspectors discovered another tank behind the build-ing that was leaking toxic waste.

    MOVED   **Behind the building**, the inspectors discovered another tank that was leaking toxic waste.

- State the word being modified.

    DANGLING   While shopping, a stuffed alligator caught my eye.

    SUBJECT ADDED While **I was** shopping, a stuffed alligator caught my eye.

- Ask, "What do I mean? Who's doing what?" Then state that directly.

    DANGLING   After debating changes in the regulations for months, the present standards were allowed to continue.
    READER'S REACTION: *Who* **is debating? Not the standards!**

    REWRITTEN   The commission debated changes in the regulations for months but decided to continue the present standards.

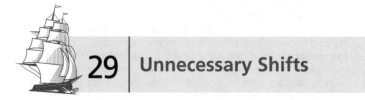

29 | Unnecessary Shifts

Especially in formal contexts, readers expect logically consistent writing.

SHIFTED	If **parents** called the school board, **we** could explain why **we** oppose the new policy.
	READER'S REACTION: I'm confused. Who should do what?
EDITED	If **parents** called the school board, **they** could explain why **they** oppose the new policy.

SERIOUS ERROR

29a Recognizing shifts in person and number

A shift in **person** occurs when you illogically switch perspective (*I* to *you* to *he* or *she*). A shift in **number** occurs when you illogically switch between singular and plural (*a person* to *they*).

INCONSISTENT	When **a business executive** is looking for a new job, **they** often consult a placement service.
	READER'S REACTION: Who is "they"? The executive?
EDITED	When **business executives are** looking for **new jobs, they** often consult a placement service.

FIRST, SECOND, AND THIRD PERSON IN THREE COMMUNITIES

- **First person singular (*I*).** Use *I* to refer to yourself as the writer or essay's subject. Readers may find *I* too personal in some formal academic contexts, especially in the sciences.
- **First person plural (*we*).** Use *we* in a collaborative project with several authors. In some academic papers, you may use *we* as you refer to ideas you and your readers share. *We* is common at work and in public when you represent or appeal to your organization.
- **Second person (*you*).** Use *you* to refer directly to the reader ("you, the reader"). In most academic and work writing, readers find *you* inappropriate, but some situations call for *you*, as in a set of instructions or a plain-language contract. In public writing that urges action, *you* can engage the reader in a civic appeal.
- **Third person (*he, she, it, they, one, someone,* and other pronouns).** Use these pronouns to refer to what you write about,

including *people, person,* and names of groups (such as *students*). Avoid sexist use of *he* and *she*. Be alert to exclusionary uses, such as pitting *we* against *they*.

SERIOUS
ERROR

29b Editing shifts in person and number

Do your nouns and pronouns refer to the same person? Are they consistently singular or plural? If not, edit for consistency.

SINGULAR   If **a student** needs loans, **he or she** should get advice.

PLURAL   If **students** need loans, **they** should get advice.

29c Recognizing shifts in tense

The **tense** of a verb indicates time as past, present, or future. When you change tense within a passage, you signal a change in time and the relationship of events. Illogical shifts can mislead your readers.

ILLOGICAL SHIFT   Scientists **discovered** nests that **indicated** how some dinosaurs **take care** of their young.

LOGICAL   Scientists **discovered** nests that **indicate** how some dinosaurs **took care** of their young.

ESL ADVICE: Verb Tense and Expressions of Time

Use consistent verb tense and time expressions to show changes in time.

INCONSISTENT   I **study** English last year, and now I **worked** for a global company.

EDITED   I **studied** English last year, and now I **work** for a global company.

29d Editing shifts in tense

Shift tense when your account or convention requires the change.

> **STRATEGY** **Match your verbs to your intended time.**

INCONSISTENT SHIFT TO PRESENT   We **had been screening** films when suddenly Jo **yells.**

EDITED   We had **been screening** films when suddenly Jo **yelled.**

Follow convention, and use present tense when you summarize or analyze events or information from a work such as a novel or film.

INCONSISTENT   As the novel begins, Ishmael **comes** to New Bedford to ship out on a whaler, which he soon **did.**

CONVENTIONAL   As the novel begins, Ishmael **comes** to New Bedford to ship out on a whaler, which he soon **does.**

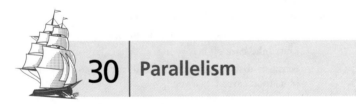

30 | Parallelism

When you use consistent patterns, readers can follow your ideas easily and concentrate on your meaning because they know what to expect. **Parallelism** is the expression of similar or related ideas in similar grammatical form; it creates sentence rhythms and highlights ideas.

WEAK   Hal furnished his apartment with what he purchased at flea markets, buying items from want ads, and gifts from friends.
READER'S REACTION: This list seems wordy and jumbled.

PARALLEL   Hal furnished his apartment with **purchases** <u>from flea mar-</u>
                 <u>kets,</u> **items** <u>from want ads</u>, and **gifts** <u>from friends</u>.

30a Recognizing faulty parallelism

Once you begin a parallel pattern, you need to complete it.

MIXED   Swimming **aids** cardiovascular fitness, **develops** overall
                 muscle strength, and **probably without causing** injuries.

PARALLEL   Swimming **aids** cardiovascular fitness, **develops** overall mus-
                 cle strength, and **causes** few injuries.

30b Editing for parallelism

Place items in a series, pair, or list using the same structure even if they
differ in length and wording. With the seven coordinating conjunctions
(*and, but, or, for, nor, so, yet*), parallelism heightens similarities or contrasts.

MIXED   A lab technician keeps a detailed notebook and the entries
                 made accurately.

PARALLEL   A lab technician keeps a **detailed and accurate** notebook.

Edit each series with the full sentence in mind. If the lead-in word can be
the same, don't repeat it. If the lead-in words differ, include them.

INCOMPLETE   The main character in the novel *Tarzan of the Apes* has
                 appeared on television, films, and comic books.

                 READER'S REACTION: I doubt he was *on* films or comic books.

EDITED   The main character in the novel *Tarzan of the Apes* has
                 appeared **on** television, **in** films, and **in** comic books.

STRATEGY   **Use parallelism to organize meaning.**

• Build up to a key point placed last in a series.

    Candidates need stamina, courage, and, most of all, **ambition.**

- List items in parallel form.

  These trends characterized the early 1960s: (a) **a growing** civil rights movement, (b) **a developing** anticommunist foreign policy, and (c) **an increasing** emphasis on youth in culture and politics.

- Connect sections of an essay or a report.

  One reason for approving this proposal now is . . .
  A second reason for acting is . . .
  The third, and most important, reason for taking steps is . . .

31 | Coordination and Subordination

Suppose you were editing a report with this passage.

California's farmers ship fresh lettuce, avocados, and other produce to supermarkets. They never send fresh olives.
READER'S REACTION: **These sentences sound choppy. How do they connect?**

Using **coordination,** you could give equal emphasis to the statements.

California's farmers ship fresh lettuce, avocados, and other produce to supermarkets**, but** they never send fresh olives.

Using **subordination,** you could show the relative weight of ideas.

California's farmers ship fresh lettuce, avocados, and other produce to supermarkets, **though** they never send fresh olives.

31a Recognizing coordination

Use coordination to link words, phrases, or clauses to emphasize their equal weight, balance the structure, or express addition or opposition.

CREATING AND PUNCTUATING COORDINATION

- Use *and, but, or, for, nor, so,* or *yet* (coordinating conjunctions). Precede them with a comma when joining two main clauses, word groups that could stand on their own as sentences (see 21a).

  cut **and** hemmed   intrigued **yet** suspicious

  The new zoning board met**,** **but** it did not vote.

- Use pairs like *either/or, neither/nor,* and *not only/but also.*

  either music therapy **or** pet therapy

- Use a semicolon.

  Some customers fidgeted**;** others stared at the ceiling.

- Use conjunctive adverbs like *however, moreover, nonetheless, thus,* and *consequently* preceded by a semicolon.

  The managers could speed up the checkout lines**;** **however,** they seldom pay much attention to the problem.

- Use a colon.

  Magazine racks by the checkout counters serve a useful purpose**:** they give customers something to read while waiting.

EXPRESSING RELATIONSHIPS THROUGH COORDINATION

RELATIONSHIP	COORDINATING CONJUNCTION	CONJUNCTIVE ADVERB
addition	, and	; in addition, ; furthermore,
opposition or contrast	, but , yet	; in contrast, ; however, ; nonetheless,
result	, so	; therefore, ; consequently,
cause	, for	
choice	, or	; otherwise
negation	, nor	

31b Recognizing subordination

Subordination creates sentences with unequal elements: the **main clause** (which could stand alone as a sentence) presents the central idea; at least one **subordinate clause** (which could not stand alone) modifies or comments on it. You signal this inequality by beginning the subordinate clause with a subordinator or relative pronoun.

CREATING AND PUNCTUATING SUBORDINATION

- **Use a subordinating conjunction** such as *although* or *because* to create a subordinate clause at the beginning (followed by a comma) or ending (after a comma if nonessential; see 34d).

  Once she understood the problem , she had no trouble solving it.

  ESSENTIAL   Radar tracking of flights began **because several air-liners collided in midair.**

  NONESSENTIAL   The present air traffic control system works reasonably well **,** **although accidents still occur.**

- **Use a relative pronoun** (*who, which, that*) to create a relative clause at the end or in the middle. Begin a clause *essential* to the meaning with *that*. Add commas only to set off nonessential detail (see 34d).

  ESSENTIAL (NO COMMA)   The anthropologists discovered the site of a building **that early settlers used as a meetinghouse.**

  NONESSENTIAL (COMMA)   On one side they found remains of a smaller building **,** **which may have been a storage shed.**

EXPRESSING RELATIONSHIPS THROUGH SUBORDINATION

RELATIONSHIP	CONJUNCTION OR OTHER WORD
Time	before, while, until, since, once, whenever
Cause	because, since
Result	in order that, so that, so, that

Concession	although, though, even though, as if, while
Place	where, wherever
Condition	if, whether, provided, unless, rather than
Comparison	as
Identification	that, which, who

31c Editing for coordination and subordination

How can you tell how much coordination or subordination to use? Read your writing aloud. Watch for short, choppy sentences or long, dense passages. Replace *and, so,* and *but* to vary or specify. Consider your community: academic readers may accept more subordination than work colleagues who favor conciseness.

STRATEGY Show what matters: Put main points in main clauses.

DRAFT His equipment was inferior, though Jim set a school record.

READER'S REACTION: **Isn't Jim's achievement the point?**

EDITED **Though** his equipment was inferior, Jim set a school record.

ESL ADVICE: Structures for Coordination and Subordination

Use both coordinators and subordinators, but don't mix the two.

MIXED **Although** frogs can live both on land and in water, **but** they need to breathe oxygen.

CONSISTENT COORDINATION Frogs can live on land and in water, **but** they need to breathe oxygen.

CONSISTENT SUBORDINATION **Although** frogs can live on land and in water, they need to breathe oxygen.

32 | Conciseness

Readers value clarity, efficiency, and directness.

WORDY   **There is evidence that the use of** pay **as an** incentive **can be a factor** in improvement **of the** quality **of** work.
           READER'S REACTION: **Why is this so long-winded?**

ABRUPT   Incentive pay improves work quality.

RESHAPED   Incentive pay **often encourages** work **of higher** quality.

32a Recognizing common types of wordiness

Unnecessary and repetitive words waste readers' time. Shrink **wordy phrases** to one or two words—or none. For example, reduce *due to the fact that* to *because* and simply drop *as a matter of fact* or *in my opinion.*

     All-purpose words like *factor, situation, type,* and *field* sound serious yet are often fillers, as are modifiers like *very, totally, major,* and *really.*

WORDY   Young Goodman Brown is **totally** overwhelmed by **his own** guilt.

CUT   Young Goodman Brown is overwhelmed by guilt.

     Redundant expressions, both pairs (*each and every*) and phrases (*large in size*), say the same thing twice. Eliminate them.

WORDY   Because it was **sophisticated in nature** and **tolerant in style,** Kublai Khan's administration aided China's development.

CUT   Because it was **sophisticated and tolerant,** Kublai Khan's administration aided China's development.

REWRITTEN   Kublai Khan's **adept and tolerant administration** aided China's development.

32b Editing for conciseness

Conciseness means using only the words you need—not the fewest possible, but only those that suit your purpose, meaning, and readers.

> **STRATEGY** **Vary your cutting and trimming.**
>
> - Cut or rewrite what you've already stated or clearly implied.
> - Reduce writer's commentary ("In my paper, I will show . . .").
> - Highlight key points in a passage that interprets or draws conclusions. Combine them as you drop generalities and add details.
> - Compress or delete word groups beginning with *which, who, that,* and *of* by converting clauses to phrases, phrases to words.
>
> | | |
> |---|---|
> | **CLAUSES** | Chavez Park, **which is an extensive facility in the center of town,** was named after Cesar Chavez, **who fought for migrant farmers' rights.** |
> | **PHRASES** | Chavez Park, **an extensive facility in the center of town,** was named after Cesar Chavez, **an advocate for migrant farmers.** |
> | **WORDS** | Chavez Park, **a downtown facility,** was named after **migrant advocate** Cesar Chavez. |

33 | Language Choices

Every speaker uses a variety of English—a **dialect**—shaped by region, culture, and home community. Where they're used, these varieties are natural. In academic, public, and work settings, however, they often are seen as "nonstandard," "incorrect," or "errors," not variations.

HOME VARIETY	Miss Brill **know** that the lovers **making** fun of her, but she **act** like she **don't** care.
EDITED	Miss Brill **knows** that the lovers **are making** fun of her, but she **acts as if** she **doesn't** care.

33a Recognizing and editing language varieties

A "rule" in one dialect may break a rule in another. In all language, the rules are structures and conventions that people in a group agree, unconsciously, to use. By **code-shifting**, you can substitute "standard edited American English" for your home language variety.

> STRATEGY **Look for "rules" in your home language.**
>
> *Rule in KY:* The lawn needs mowed
>
> *Rule elsewhere:* The lawn needs <u>to be</u> mowed.

33b Recognizing and editing disrespectful language

Treat others fairly by eliminating sexist and discriminatory language. Avoid using *he, him,* or *men* for all people and implying men in occupations (*firemen*).

SEXIST	Every trainee brought **his** laptop with **him**.
AWKWARD	Every trainee brought **his or her** laptop with **him or her**.
BETTER	All trainees brought **their** laptops with **them**.

Most readers won't tolerate unfair biases against groups of people.

DEMEANING	My paper focuses on the **weird** courtship rituals of a **barbaric** Aboriginal tribe in southwestern Australia.
	READER'S REACTION: Your paper sounds biased. How can you treat this topic fairly if you don't respect the tribe?
EDITED	My paper focuses on the unique courtship rituals of an Aboriginal tribe in southwestern Australia.

PART

6

Writing with Conventions

Voices
from the Community

"Parenthetical remarks (however relevant) are unnecessary."

—Frank L. Visco, *How to Write Good*

34 | Commas

Because a comma can join, separate, or disrupt, it's easy to misuse. Public and work communities that favor direct prose may expect the fewest commas, while academic readers are likely to expect formal comma usage.

CONFUSING   During the study interviews were used to gather responses from participants, and to supplement written artifacts.
          READER'S REACTION: I can't tell where ideas begin and end.

EDITED   During the study **,** interviews were used to gather responses from participants and to supplement written artifacts.

SERIOUS ERROR
34a Recognizing commas that join sentences

When you use *and, but, or, for, nor, so,* or *yet* (**coordinating conjunctions**) to link two word groups that can stand alone as sentences, place a comma *before* the conjunction. (Avoid a comma splice. See 22a.)

DRAFT   The rain soaked the soil and the mud buried the road.
EDITED   The rain soaked the soil **,** **and** the mud buried the road.

SERIOUS ERROR
34b Editing commas that join sentences

Analyze the pair joined by a conjunction. If you find main clauses that could stand alone before and after the conjunction, add a comma *before* the conjunction. Even to join short main clauses, a comma is always acceptable but might be omitted informally.

Apex tried to ship the order **,** **but** the truck was late.

Do *not* separate any other pair with a comma.

We **sanded** and **stained** the old table.

I used stain that was **cheap** and **easy to clean.**

SERIOUS ERROR

34c Recognizing commas that set off sentence elements

The simplest sentences need no comma. Add commas to set off expressions that introduce or interrupt a sentence with interesting detail.

noun phrase	verb phrase
The storm	developed quickly.

INTRODUCTORY	**For nearly an hour,** the rain drenched Old Town.
TRANSITION	**In addition,** the hail caused damage.
INTERRUPTER	It broke, **I think,** a dozen church windows.
CONJUNCTIVE ADVERB	We hope, **therefore,** that someone starts a repair fund.
TAG QUESTION	We'll contribute, **won't we?**
CONTRAST	The windows' beauty touches all of us, **not just the church members.**
DIRECT ADDRESS	Recall, **friends of beauty,** that every gift helps.
NONRESTRICTIVE MODIFIER	The stained glass, **glowing like exotic jewels,** enriches us all.

SERIOUS ERROR

34d Editing commas that set off sentence elements

Use two commas to enclose an expression in midsentence; use just one after an opening or before a closing expression.

Introductory elements. Readers expect a comma to signal where the introduction ends and the main sentence begins.

CONFUSING	Forgetting to alert the media before the rally Jessica rushed to the park.
EDITED	Forgetting to alert the media before the rally , Jessica rushed to the park.

In general, put a comma after a long introductory element following a sub-ordinating conjunction (*although, because, when;* see 31b), a preposition (*during, without, between*), or a verbal (*to live, living, lived*). Add a comma if a short introductory element might confuse readers.

CONFUSING	By six boats began showing up.
EDITED	By six , boats began showing up.

Parenthetical expressions. Use commas to help readers identify word groups that interrupt a sentence.

DRAFT	Teams should meet even spontaneously as needed.
EDITED	Teams should meet , even spontaneously , as needed.

Nonessential, nonrestrictive modifiers. Midsentence modifiers act as adjectives or adverbs, adding detail that qualifies other words.

STRATEGY   **Test whether a modifier is essential.**

Drop the modifier, and see whether the essential meaning of the sentence stays the same. If it does, even if it's less informative, the modifier is **nonrestrictive,** adding detail that's interesting or useful but not necessary for meaning. Set it off *with* commas so readers see it as nonessential.

DRAFT	Their band **which performs in small clubs** has gotten fine reviews.
	TEST: Their band has gotten fine reviews. [The meaning is the same though it's less informative.]
COMMAS ADDED (NONRESTRICTIVE)	Their band , **which performs in small clubs ,** has gotten fine reviews.

If dropping a modifier eliminates essential information and changes the meaning of the sentence, the modifier is **restrictive.** Add it *without* commas so readers see it as a necessary part of the sentence.

DRAFT	The charts **,** **drawn by hand,** were hard to read.
	TEST: The charts were hard to read. [This says *all* the charts were hard to read but means that only *some* were.]
COMMAS OMITTED (RESTRICTIVE)	The charts **drawn by hand** were hard to read.

Who, which, and *that.* Add commas to set off nonrestrictive (nonessential) clauses beginning with *who, which, whom, whose, when,* or *where.* Because *that* can specify, rather than add, use it in restrictive (essential) clauses. *Which* often begins nonessentials but can be used either way.

NONRESTRICTIVE	Preventive dentistry **,** **which is receiving great emphasis,** may reduce visits to the dentist's office.
RESTRICTIVE	Dentists **who encourage good hygiene** give advice.
RESTRICTIVE	They supply samples **that encourage good habits.**

Appositives. An **appositive,** a noun or pronoun that renames a preceding noun, is usually nonrestrictive (nonessential). If so, add commas.

NONRESTRICTIVE	Amy Nguyen **,** **a poet from Vietnam,** published another collection of verse.
RESTRICTIVE	The well-known executive **Louis Gerstner** went from RJR Nabisco to IBM.

SERIOUS ERROR 34e Editing disruptive commas

Unless you need to set off an intervening expression, you'll irritate readers if a comma separates subject and predicate.

SPLIT SUBJECT AND PREDICATE	The painting *Rocks at L'Estaque* **,** is in the Museu de Arte.
EDITED	The **painting** *Rocks at L'Estaque* **is** in the Museu de Arte.

Subordinating conjunctions (such as *because;* see 31b) shouldn't be followed by commas because they introduce entire clauses. Don't mistake them for conjunctive adverbs (such as *however;* see 31a) or transitional expressions (such as *for example*), which should be set off with commas.

EXTRA COMMA   Although, Jewel lost her luggage, she had her laptop.

EDITED   **Although** Jewel lost her luggage, she had her laptop.

SERIOUS ERROR

34f Editing commas with words in a series

Use commas to separate or relate items in a series.

Series of three or more. To avoid ambiguity, consistently use commas between all items of roughly equal status, even if an item has multiple parts. Although readers in the academic community frequently expect the comma just before *and,* it's often omitted, especially in a short, clear list.

The Human Relations Office has forms for medical benefits, dental and vision options, **and** retirement contributions.

Numbered or lettered list. Punctuate a list in a sentence like a series; when items contain commas, separate them with semicolons (see 35c).

You should (a) measure the water's salinity, (b) weigh any waste in the filter, and (c) determine the amount of dissolved oxygen.

Adjectives in sequence. When you use **coordinate adjectives,** each modifies the noun (or pronoun) on its own. Separate them with commas to show their equal application to the noun. When you use **noncoordinate adjectives,** one modifies the other, and it, in turn, modifies the noun (or pronoun). Don't separate these adjectives with a comma.

STRATEGY Ask questions about adjectives.

If you answer with *yes*, the adjectives are coordinate. Use a comma.

- Can you place *and* or *but* between the adjectives?

  COORDINATE (EQUAL)   Irrigation has turned dry, infertile [*dry and infertile?—yes*] land into orchards.

  NOT COORDINATE   The funds went to new computer [*new and computer?—no*] equipment.

- Is the sense the same if you reverse the adjectives?

  COORDINATE (EQUAL)   We left our small, cramped [*cramped small?—yes, the same*] office.

  NOT COORDINATE   We bought a red brick [*brick red?—no, could mean a color*] building.

COMMA CONVENTIONS

DATES

on Friday, May 4, 2007   5 April 1973   October 2001

NUMBERS

1,746 sheep (or 1746 sheep) $8,543,234   page 2054

ADDRESSES AND PLACE NAMES IN SENTENCES

in Chicago   in Chicago, Illinois, during May

Fredelle Seed Brokers, Box 389, Holland, MI 30127

PEOPLE'S NAMES AND TITLES

Shamoon, Linda   Cris Burk, A.I.A., was the designer.

OPENINGS AND CLOSINGS OF LETTERS

PERSONAL   Dear Nan,   Dear Soccer Team,   Regards,

BUSINESS OR FORMAL   Dear Ms. Yun: Sincerely,

35 | Semicolons and Colons

Semicolons and colons help readers understand connections.

TWO SENTENCES   On April 12, 1861, one of Beauregard's batteries fired on Fort **Sumter• The** Civil War had begun.
READER'S REACTION: These sentences may present facts or drama, but they don't *necessarily* connect events.

SEMICOLON   On April 12, 1861, one of Beauregard's batteries fired on Fort **Sumter; the** Civil War had begun.
READER'S REACTION: The semicolon encourages me to link the battery firing to the Civil War beginning.

COLON   On April 12, 1861, one of Beauregard's batteries fired on Fort **Sumter: the** Civil War had begun.
READER'S REACTION: Now I see the guns' firing as a dramatic moment: the beginning of the Civil War.

35a Recognizing semicolons that join sentences

A semicolon can dramatically highlight a close relationship or a contrast.

TWO SENTENCES   Demand for paper is at an all-time high• Business alone consumes millions of tons each year.

ONE SENTENCE WITH SEMICOLON   Demand for paper is at an all-time high; business alone consumes millions of tons each year.

35b Editing semicolons that join sentences

Using a semicolon alone to link main clauses assumes a reader can figure out how they relate. Adding words specifies the connection. You can choose a **conjunctive adverb** (*thus, moreover;* see 31a) or a **transitional expression** (*for example, in contrast, on the other hand*).

Assertion **;** ⟶ transition **,** ⟶ assertion

I like apples **;** **however ,** I hate pears.

Vary the punctuation depending on where you place such wording.

BETWEEN CLAUSES   Joe survived the flood **;** **however ,** Al was never found.

WITHIN CLAUSE   Joe survived the flood **;** Al **,** **however ,** was never found.

AT END OF CLAUSE   Joe survived the flood **;** Al was never found **,** **however.**

35c Editing semicolons in a complex series

When items in a series contain commas, readers may have trouble deciding which commas separate parts of the series and which belong within items. To avoid confusion, put semicolons between such items.

I met Debbie Rios, the attorney **;** Rhonda Marron, the accountant **;** and the new financial director.

35d Recognizing and editing colons

A colon effectively joins main clauses when the second clause focuses, sums up, or illustrates the first.

COLON WITH MAIN CLAUSES   The blizzard swept the prairie **:** the Oregon Trail was closed.

The words *before* the colon generally form a complete sentence while those after—the example, list, or quotation—may or may not.

COLON WITH LIST   The symptoms are as follows **:** cough, fever, and pain.

When you introduce a list with a word group other than a complete sentence, do not use a colon.

DRAFT	Her pastimes were **:** walking, volunteering, and cooking.
EDITED	Her pastimes **were walking,** volunteering, and cooking.
EDITED	**She had three pastimes:** walking, volunteering, and cooking.

Whether a quotation is integrated with your words or set off as a block (see 16d), a sentence must precede a colon. If not, use a comma.

| **COLON WITH QUOTATION** | Dan answered his critics **:** "Sales are up and costs down." |

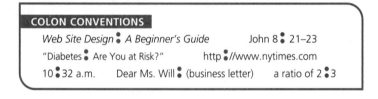

COLON CONVENTIONS

Web Site Design **:** *A Beginner's Guide*   John 8 **:** 21–23

"Diabetes **:** Are You at Risk?"   http **:**//www.nytimes.com

10 **:** 32 a.m.   Dear Ms. Will **:** (business letter)   a ratio of 2 **:** 3

36 | Apostrophes

Like the dot above the *i,* the apostrophe may seem trivial, but without it, readers would stumble over your text.

MISUSED OR LEFT OUT	Though its an 1854 novel, Dickens *Hard Times* remain's an ageless critique of education by fact's.
	READER'S REACTION: I can't tell possessives from contractions and plurals in this sentence.
EDITED	Though it **'**s an 1854 novel, Dickens **'**s *Hard Times* **remains** an ageless critique of education by **facts.**

36a Recognizing apostrophes that mark possession

Nouns that express ownership are called **possessive nouns.** Mark them to distinguish them from plurals.

**APOSTROPHE
MISSING**

The cat⬚s meow is becoming fainter.

> **READER'S REACTION: I expected "The cats meow all night." Do you mean many cats or the meow of one cat?**

**APOSTROPHE
ADDED**

The **cat's** meow is becoming fainter.

STRATEGY Test a noun for possession.

If you can turn it into an *of* phrase, use a possessive. If not, use a plural.

DRAFT

The officers reports surprised the reporters.

> **TEST: The reports *of* the officers? [*yes; possessive*]**
> **TEST: Surprised *of* the reporters? [*no; plural*]**

EDITED

The officers' reports surprised the reporters.

36b Editing apostrophes that mark possession

Decide what to add: ' + *-s* or just '.

STRATEGY Check the ending of the noun.

- **Does the noun end in a letter other than *-s*? Add ' + s.**

  Ohio'**s** taxes   the dog'**s** collar   women'**s** track

- **Does the noun end in *-s*, and is it plural? Add '.**

  the Solomons' car   buses' routes

- **Does the noun end in *-s*, and is it singular?**

  **OPTION #1
  (PREFERRED)**   Add ' + *-s*: Chris'**s** van

  OPTION #2   Add ' *after* the final *-s*: Chris' van

- **Does the noun end in -s and sound awkward?**

OPTION #1	Hodges's (sounds awkward as "Hodges-es")
	Add ' but no -s: Hodges' (shows one -s sound)
OPTION #2	Change the construction.
DRAFT	the Adams County Schools's policy
EDITED	the policy of the Adams County Schools

Decide whether nouns joined by *and* or *or* act separately or together.

| SEPARATE LAWYERS | **Bo's and Hal's** lawyers are ruthless. |
| SINGLE LEGAL TEAM | **Bo and Hal's** lawyers are ruthless. |

APOSTROPHE CONVENTIONS

Dates   the '90s   the class of '05   1980s

Plural Letters and Numbers   p's and q's   size 10's

Abbreviations   IQs   TAs

Dialect   I'm **a-goin'** for some **o'** them shrimp.

Hyphenated Noun   My **father-in-law's** library is huge.

Multiword Noun   The **union leaders'** talks collapsed.

36c Recognizing apostrophes that mark contractions

Informally, use an apostrophe to mark omitted letters when words are combined in a **contraction** (can't = can + not). In most academic writing, avoid splicing nouns with contractions (Zorr's testing = Zorr is testing).

36d Editing apostrophes that mark contractions

Some confusing contractions sound like other words.

they're = they + are   there = adverb

who's = who + is   whose = possessive pronoun

STRATEGY Expand contractions to test the form.

DRAFT   **Its** the best animal shelter in **its** area.

EXPANSION TEST: *It is [yes, a fit]* the best animal shelter in *it is [no, not a fit]* area.

EDITED   **It⁹s** the best animal shelter in **its** area.

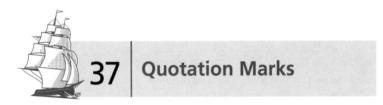

37 | Quotation Marks

Quotation marks set off someone else's spoken or written words.

DRAFT   "Without the navigator," the pilot said, we would have crashed.

READER'S REACTION: **Without quotation marks, I didn't realize that the pilot said the last part, too.**

EDITED   **66**Without the navigator,**99** the pilot said, **66**we would have crashed.**99**

SERIOUS ERROR 37a Recognizing marks that set off quotations

When you quote *directly,* use double quotation marks (" ") around the exact words quoted. (See 16d and 37b.) In dialogue, use new marks and indent when a new person speaks.

DIRECT   **66**The loon can stay under water for several minutes,**99**
QUOTATION   the ranger told us.
(SPOKEN)

DIRECT QUOTATION (WRITTEN)   Gross argues that "every generation scorns its off-spring's culture" (9).

DIRECT QUOTATION INTERRUPTED   "Every generation," Gross claims, "scorns its off-spring's culture" (9).

ESL ADVICE: Quotation Marks

Check for American conventions if your native language uses other marks for quotations or if you are used to British conventions. Search for these marks with your computer to spot unconventional usage.

SERIOUS ERROR   ## 37b   Editing marks that set off quotations

When one quotation contains another, use single marks (' ') for the inside quotation and double marks (" ") for the one enclosing it.

QUOTATION INSIDE QUOTATION   De Morga's account described the battle that "caused his ship to 'burst asunder' " (Goddio 37).

For quotation marks for emphasis, see 38b. For *indirect* quotations that paraphrase or sum up someone's words, omit quotation marks. (See 16a.)

SUMMARY (INDIRECT)   De Morga brings the battle to life (Goddio 37).

COMBINING MARKS

- Position commas to help readers distinguish your introduction, commentary, or source from the quotation. (See also 44h.)

   "Our unity , " said the mayor , "is our strength."

- If your words end with *that*, don't include a comma.

   Some claimed that "calamity followed Jane." Jane replied that she simply outran it.

- Place these marks *inside* concluding single or double quotation marks: commas, periods, and question or exclamation marks that are part of the quoted material. Place these marks *outside:* semicolons, colons, and question or exclamation marks that apply to the whole sentence.

37c Editing quotation marks with titles of short works

Use quotation marks for titles of short works and parts of larger works.

CONVENTIONS FOR TITLES

ITALICS OR UNDERLINING	QUOTATION MARKS
BOOK, NOVEL, COLLECTION *The Labyrinth of Solitude*	**CHAPTER, ESSAY, SELECTION** "The Day of the Dead"
PAMPHLET *Guide for Surgery Patients*	**SECTION** "Anesthesia"
LONG POEM *Paradise Lost* *The One Day*	**SHORT POEM, FIRST LINE TITLE** "Richard Cory" "Whoso list to hunt"
RADIO, TV PROGRAM *The West Wing*	**EPISODE, REPORT** "Gone Quiet"
MUSICAL WORK, ALBUM *Invisible Touch* *Organ Symphony* BUT Symphony no. 3 in C Minor, op. 78	**SECTION, SONG** "Big Money"
MAGAZINE, NEWSPAPER, JOURNAL *Discover* *Composition Review*	**ARTICLE** "What Can Baby Learn?" "Student Revision Practices"
PLAY, FILM, ART WORK *King Lear*	**UNPUBLISHED WORK, LECTURE** "Renaissance Women"

NO ITALICS, UNDERLINING, OR QUOTATION MARKS

SACRED BOOKS, PUBLIC OR LEGAL DOCUMENTS

Bible, Koran, Talmud, United States Constitution

TITLE OF YOUR OWN PAPER (UNLESS PUBLISHED)

The Theme of the Life Voyage in Crane's "Open Boat"

The Role of Verbal Abuse in The Color Purple

38 | Italics and Underlining

Italic type slants to the right and emphasizes words. Underlining (handwritten or typed) is its equivalent: The Color Purple = *The Color Purple*. Many college teachers prefer underlining because it's easy to see.

UNDERLINING   Alice Walker's novel The Color Purple has been praised and criticized since 1982.`

READER'S REACTION: I can spot the title right away.

38a Recognizing conventions for italics (underlining)

Italicize titles of most long, complete works (see 37c). Italicize names of specific ships, planes, trains, and spacecraft (*Voyager VI, Orient Express*) but not *types* of vehicles (Boeing 767) or *USS* and *SS* (USS *Corpus Christi*). Italicize uncommon foreign expressions (*omertà*) but not common ones (junta, taco). Italicize scientific names for plants (*Chrodus crispus*) and animals (*Gazella dorcas*) but not common names (seaweed, gazelle).

38b Editing for conventions that show emphasis

Use italics to focus on a term or a word, letter, or number as itself.

In Boston, *r* is pronounced *ah* so that *car* becomes *cah*.

Set off technical or unusual terms with quotation marks or italics.

In real estate, **"**FSBO**"** (pronounced **"**fizbo**"**) refers to a home that is **"**for sale by owner.**"**

You can—*sparingly*—use italics for emphasis or contrast or use quotation marks for irony, sarcasm, or distance from a term.

| **INFORMAL** | <u>Hand</u> the receipts to me. |
| **MORE FORMAL** | Give the receipts to me personally. |

39 | Capitals

Readers expect capital letters to signal sentences or specific names.

CAPITALS MISSING	thanks, ahmed, for your file. i'll review it by tuesday.
	READER'S REACTION: Email or not, this is distracting.
CAPITALS IN PLACE	**T**hanks, **A**hmed, for your file. **I**'ll review it by **T**uesday.

39a Recognizing capitals that begin sentences

Capital letters begin both sentences and partial sentences (see 21c).

Pack for Yellowstone this July. **W**ildlife and wonders galore!

39b Editing capitals that begin sentences

When capitals are flexible, be consistent within a text. Especially in the academic community, capitalize the first word in a quotation that is a complete sentence or that begins your sentence.

| **SENTENCE QUOTED** | According to Galloway, "**T**he novel opens with an unusual chapter" (18). |

Don't capitalize part of a quotation integrated into your sentence structure or interrupted by your own words.

INTEGRATED   Galloway finds the opening "**a**n unusual chapter" (18).

INTERRUPTED   "**T**he novel," claims Galloway, "**o**pens with an unusual chapter" (18).

Sentence in parentheses. Capitalize the first word of a sentence that stands on its own, but not one placed *inside* another sentence.

FREESTANDING   By this time, the Union forces were split into nineteen sections. (**E**ven so, Grant was determined to unite them.)

ENCLOSED   Saskatchewan depends on farming (**t**he province produces over half of Canada's wheat), oil, and mining.

First word in a line of poetry. Traditionally, lines of poetry begin with capitals, but follow the poet's practice.

We said goodbye at the barrier,

And she slipped away. . . .

Robert Daseler, "At the Barrier," *Levering Avenue*

Questions in a series. Capitalize or lowercase the series.

OPTION #1   Do we need posters? **S**igns? **F**lyers?

OPTION #2   Do we need posters? **s**igns? **f**lyers?

Sentence after a colon. If a *sentence* follows a colon, choose capitals or lowercase. Otherwise, do not use a capital.

OPTION #1   The province is bilingual: **O**ne-third speak French.

OPTION #2   The province is bilingual: **o**ne-third speak French.

Run-in list. When a list is presented on text lines, don't capitalize.

NOT CAPITALIZED   Include costs for (a) **l**abs, (b) **p**hones, and (c) **s**upplies.

Vertical list. Capitalize sentences in vertical lists. Choose whether to capitalize word groups in an outline without periods.

OPTION #1 1. **L**ab facilities   **OPTION #2** 1. **l**ab facilities

2. **E**quipment   2. **e**quipment

39c Editing capitals that begin words

Capitalize names of specific people, places, and things (**proper nouns**) as well as related **proper adjectives:** Brazil, Brazilian music.

In titles, capitalize first and last words, and all words between *except* articles (*a, an, the*), prepositions under five letters (*of, to*), and coordinating conjunctions (*and, but*). Capitalize the word after any colon.

The Mill on the Floss   "Civil Rights: What Now?"

Building a Small Business (your own title)

In an APA reference list, capitalize only proper nouns and the first letters of titles and subtitles of full works (see 18b).

CAPITALIZATION CONVENTIONS

CAPITALS	LOWERCASE
INDIVIDUALS, PEOPLE, LANGUAGES	
Georgia O'Keeffe, Mother	my cousin, her dad
Maori, African American	the language, the people
TIME PERIODS, SEASONS, EVENTS	
October, Ramadan	spring, winter, holiday
Jazz Age, Postmodernism	the movement, a trend
RELIGIONS, RELATED SUBJECTS	
Talmud, Bible, God	talmudic, biblical, a god

CAPITALS	LOWERCASE
ORGANIZATIONS, INSTITUTIONS, COURSES	
U.S. Senate	a senator
Air Line Pilots Association	the union, a union member
Harbor Community College	a university, the college
Sociology 203, Art 101	a philosophy course
PLACES, REGIONS, BUILDINGS	
Malaysia, the Southwest	the country, southwestern
Taj Mahal, Getty Museum	the tower, a bridge
NAMES AND TERMS	
Siemens, Kleenex, Voyager	the company, tissues, van
Big Dipper, Earth (planet)	star, earth (ground)

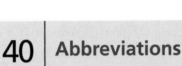

40 | Abbreviations

When they are accepted by both writer and reader, abbreviations act as a kind of shorthand, making a sentence easy to write and read.

CONFUSING   **Jg. Rich.** Paret was a **U of C** law **prof.**

                 READER'S REACTION: What's "U of C"—University of California?

CLEAR   **Judge Richard** Paret was a **University of Chicago** law **professor.**

40a   Recognizing and editing abbreviations

Titles with proper names. Abbreviate a title just before or after a person's name. Use one form of a title at a time. Abbreviated academic titles (*M.A., Ph.D., B.S., M.D.*) can be used on their own or after a name.

Jack Gill, **Sr.**   **Dr.** Vi McGee   Vi McGee, **D.D.S.**

Spell out the title if it's part of your reference to the person or if it does not appear next to a proper name.

Professor Drew   Prof. Ann Drew   NOT Prof. Drew

Exceptions: Rev. Mills   Dr. Smith

ESL ADVICE: Abbreviated Titles

If titles such as *Dr.* or *Mrs.* do not require periods in your first language as they do in English, proofread carefully.

People and groups. Readers accept familiar (IBM), simple (AFL-CIO), or standard (FAFSA) abbreviations. Most use capitals without periods.

ORGANIZATIONS	NAACP, AMA, GM, CNN, 3M
COUNTRIES	USA (*or* U.S.A.), UK (*or* U.K.)
PEOPLE OR THINGS	JFK, LBJ, FDR, MLK, TB, AWOL, DUI

STRATEGY Introduce an unfamiliar abbreviation.

Give the full expression when you first use it, and show the abbreviation in parentheses. Then, use just the abbreviation.

The **American Library Association (ALA)** studies policy on information access. The **ALA** also opposes censorship.

Dates and numbers. Abbreviations ($, *no.* for number) may be used with *specific* dates, numbers, or amounts.

BC; BCE	*before Christ; before common era* (alternative for BC)
AD	*anno Domini,* "in the year of Our Lord"
CE	Common Era (alternative for AD)
a.m. or A.M.	*ante meridiem,* "before noon" (A.M. in print)
p.m. or P.M.	*post meridiem,* "after noon" (P.M. in print)

40b Editing to use abbreviations sparingly

In research, scientific, technical, or specialized contexts, such as documenting sources, you can abbreviate more than in formal text.

CONVENTIONS FOR ABBREVIATIONS

- **In formal writing**

  Thursday, not Thurs.   Walton Avenue, not Ave.

  Exception: 988 Red Road, Paramus, NJ 07652

  physical education   quart   mile   kilogram   chapter

  Exceptions: rpm, mph (with or without periods)
- **In tables or graphs: @, #, =, −, +,** other symbols
- **In documentation:** ch.   p.   pp.   fig.
- **In documentation and parentheses (from Latin)**

  e.g.: for example (*exempli gratia*)   i.e.: that is (*id est*)
  et al.: and others (*et alii*)   etc.: and so forth (*et cetera*)

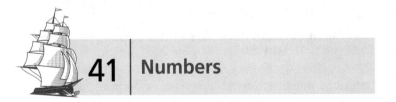

41 | Numbers

You can convey numbers with numerals (37, 18.6), words (fifteen, two million), or a combination (7th, 2nd, 25 billion). Follow the advice here for numbers in general writing. In technical, business, and scientific contexts, follow conventional and consistent usage.

CONVENTIONS FOR NUMBERS IN GENERAL TEXT

- **Addresses and Routes**

  Interstate 6   2450 Ridge Road, Alhambra, CA 91801

- **Dates**

September 7, 1976	1880–1910	from 1955 to 1957
1960s	the sixties	the '60s (informal)
nineteenth century	AD (or CE) 980	class of '05

- **Times of Day**

10:52 6:17 a.m.	12 p.m. (noon)	12 a.m. (midnight)
four in the morning	four o'clock	half past eight

- **Parts of a Written Work**

  Chapter 12

  Genesis 1:1–6 or Gen.1.1–6 (MLA style)

  Macbeth 2.4.25–28 (or act II, scene iv, lines 25–28)

- **Measurements, Fractions, Decimals, Statistics**

120 MB	55 mph	6'4"	47 psi
21 ml	7 $\frac{5}{8}$	27.3	67 percent (or 67%)
7 out of 10	3 to 1	won 5 to 4	a mean of 23

- **Money**

  $7,883 $4.29 $7.2 million (or $7,200,000)

- **Rounded**

  75 million years   three hundred thousand voters

- **Ranges:** Simply supply the last two figures in the second number unless readers will need more to avoid confusion.

  34–45   95–102 (not 95–02)   370–420   1534–620

- **Ranges of Years:** Supply all digits for different centuries.

  1890–1920   1770–86   476–823   42–38 BC

- **Clusters:** items 2, 5, and 8 through 10 (or 8–10)

GENERAL TEXT	These **fifty-two** chemists represent **thirty** labs.
	READER'S REACTION: **In general academic texts, I expect most numbers to be spelled out.**
TECHNICAL	These **52** chemists represent **30** labs.
	READER'S REACTION: **In technical papers, I expect more figures.**

41a Recognizing when to spell or use numerals

In general, spell out numbers composed of one or two words, treating hyphenated compounds as a single word.

ten books   **twenty-seven** computers   **306** employees

41b Editing numbers in general text

Treat comparable numbers in a passage consistently as words or numerals (for all if required for one). Spell opening numbers, or rewrite.

CONSISTENT	Café Luna's menu soon expanded from **85** to **104** items.

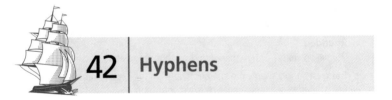

42 | Hyphens

Hyphens both join and divide words. Type a hyphen as a *single* line (-) with no space on either side: well-trained engineer, not well - trained engineer.

CONFUSING	The Japanese language proposal is well prepared.
	READER'S REACTION: **Is the proposal *in* or *about* Japanese?**
CLARIFIED	The Japanese-language proposal is well prepared.

42a   Recognizing hyphens that join words

A **compound word** is made of two or more words hyphenated (*double-decker*), spelled as one (*timekeeper*), or treated as separate (*letter carrier*). Compounds change rapidly; observe community practice.

42b   Editing hyphens that join words

Numbers. In general (not technical) writing, hyphenate numbers between twenty-one and ninety-nine (even if part of a larger one), inclusive numbers, and fractions: *fifty ▬one thousand, volumes 9 ▬14, two ▬thirds*.

Prefixes and suffixes. Hyphenate a prefix before a capital or number and with *ex-, self-, all-, -elect,* and *-odd: pre ▬1989, self ▬centered*.

Letters with words. Hyphenate a letter and a word forming a compound, except in music terms: *A ▬frame, T ▬shirt, A minor, G sharp*.

Confusing words. Use hyphens to distinguish words with the same spelling (*recreation, re ▬creation*) or repeated letters (*post ▬traumatic*).

Compound modifiers. When two or more words work as a single modifier, generally hyphenate them *before* but not *after* a noun.

BEFORE NOUN (-)   Many **nausea ▬inducing** drugs treat cancer.

AFTER NOUN (NO -)   Many drugs that treat cancer are **nausea inducing**.

Do not hyphenate with *-ly* adverbs (highly regarded staff) or comparative forms (more popular products).

42c   Editing hyphens that divide words

Word processors can automatically hyphenate words at the end of a line but often create hard-to-read lines or incorrectly split words. As a result, many writers turn off this feature (as MLA and APA suggest). When you must divide an electronic address, do so after a slash. Don't add a hyphen.

43 | Spelling

Readers may laugh at a newspaper misspelling but harshly judge a writer who misspells in an academic paper or work document.

INCORRECT The city will not **except** any late bids.

> READER'S REACTION: I get annoyed when careless or lazy writers won't correct their spelling!

PROOFREAD The city will not **accept** any late bids.

43a Using the computer to proofread for spelling

When you use a spelling checker, the computer compares each word in your text with the words in its dictionary. If it finds a match, it assumes your word is correct. If it does *not* find a match, it asks you if the word is misspelled. It can't identify words correctly spelled but used incorrectly (*lead* or *led*).

43b Recognizing and editing spelling errors

Correct errors you see; ask readers to help you spot others.

> **STRATEGY** Go beyond the spelling checker.
>
> - Say the word carefully. Look up possible spellings, even odd ones. If you reach the right area in a dictionary, you may find the word.
> - Try a dictionary for poor spellers that lists correct spellings (*phantom*) and likely misspellings (*fantom*).
> - Try a thesaurus; the word may be listed as a synonym.
> - Ask others for technical terms; verify their advice in a dictionary.
> - Check the indexes of books on the word's topic.
> - Look for the word in textbooks, company materials, or newspapers.

- Add a tricky word to your own spelling list. Invent a way to remember it (associating the two *z*'s in *quizzes* with boredom—*zzzzzz*).
- Identify spelling patterns that will help you avoid errors—such as *i* before *e* except after *c* or when sounding like *a*.
- Check confusing words in the Glossary (pp. 233–50).

44 | Other Marks and Conventions

You can use punctuation marks to change the style and sense of your prose as you set boundaries, guide readers, and add emphasis.

DASHES
The boy—**clutching his allowance**—came to the store.
READER'S REACTION: Dashes show strong emphasis; I can tell how hard the boy worked to save his money.

PARENTHESES
The boy (**clutching his allowance**) came to the store.
READER'S REACTION: Parentheses deemphasize his savings, thus giving his arrival more significance.

COMMAS
The boy, **clutching his allowance**, came to the store.
READER'S REACTION: This direct account doesn't emphasize either the savings or the arrival.

44a Recognizing and editing parentheses

Parentheses *enclose:* You can't use just one, and readers will interpret whatever falls between the pair as an aside.

Sign up for Telepick (including Internet access) and get free calls.

When parentheses *inside a sentence* end it, punctuate *after* the closing mark. When they enclose a *freestanding sentence,* punctuate *inside* the mark.

INSIDE SENTENCE   People on your list get discounts (once they sign up).

SEPARATE SENTENCE   Try Telepick now. (This offer excludes international calls.)

You can use parentheses to mark numbered or lettered lists.

NUMBERED LIST   Fax Harry's Bookstore (555–0934) to (1) order books, (2) inquire about items, or (3) sign up for events.

44b Recognizing and editing dashes

Too many may strike academic readers as informal, but dashes can add flair to work and public appeals, ads, or brochures. Type a dash as two unspaced hyphens, without space before or after: --. A print dash appears as a single line: —. Use one dash with an idea or series that opens or ends a sentence; use a pair to enclose words in the middle.

OPENING LIST   **Extended visiting hours, better meals, and more exercise**—these were the inmates' demands.

PAIR IN THE MIDDLE   For her service to two groups—**Kids First and Food Basket**—Olivia was voted Volunteer of the Year.

44c Recognizing and editing brackets

Academic readers expect you to use brackets scrupulously (though other readers may find them pretentious). When you add your words to a quotation for clarity or background, bracket this **interpolation.** Also bracket *sic* (Latin for "thus") after a source error to confirm your accuracy.

INTERPOLATION   As Walz notes, "When Catholic Europe adopted the new Gregorian calendar in 1582, Protestant England still followed October 4 by October 5 [Julian calendar]" (4).

44d Recognizing and editing ellipses

The **ellipsis** is three *spaced* periods that mark where something has been left out. Academic readers expect ellipses to mark omissions of irrelevant material from quotations; other readers may prefer full quotations.

CONVENTIONS FOR ELLIPSIS MARKS

- Use three spaced periods • • • for ellipses in a sentence or within a line of poetry.
- Use a period before an ellipsis ending a sentence• • • •
- Leave a space before the first period • • • and after the last unless the ellipsis is bracketed.
- Omit ellipses when you begin quotations (unless needed for clarity) or use clearly incomplete words or phrases.
- Retain another punctuation mark before omitted words if needed for the sentence structure; • • • omit it otherwise.
- Supply a series of spaced periods (MLA style) to show an omitted line (or more) of poetry in a block quotation.
- When quoting a text that uses ellipses, bracket your ellipses $\left[\, • \, • \, • \,\right]$ in MLA style if necessary to avoid confusion.

When you drop *part* of a sentence, maintain normal sentence structure so readers can follow the passage.

INTERVIEW NOTES   Museum Director: "We expect the Inca pottery in our special exhibit to attract historians from as far away as Chicago, while the vivid jewelry draws the public."

CONFUSING DRAFT   The museum director hopes "the Inca pottery • • • historians • • • vivid jewelry • • • public."

EDITED   The museum director "expect[s] the Inca pottery • • • to attract historians • • • while the vivid jewelry draws the public."

44e Recognizing and editing slashes

You can use a slash to mark alternatives (the **on/off** switch), especially in technical documents, but readers may find it informal or imprecise (preferring *or* instead). When you quote poetry *within* your text, separate lines of verse with a slash, typing a space before and after.

> The speaker in Sidney's sonnet hails the moon: "O Moon, thou climb'st the skies! **/** How silently . . ." (lines 1–2).

44f Recognizing and editing end marks

Speakers change pitch or pause to mark sentence boundaries. Writers use symbols—period, question mark, exclamation point.

LESS FORMAL	Why do we need you? You help our pups find families!
	READER'S REACTION: This bouncy style is great for the volunteer brochure but not the annual report.
MORE FORMAL	The League's volunteers remain our most valuable asset, matching abandoned animals with suitable homes.

Periods. All sentences that are *statements* end with periods—even if they contain embedded clauses that report, rather than ask, questions. Periods also mark decimal points (5●75) and abbreviations (Dr●, Ms●, pp●, etc●, a●m●) though many abbreviations, pronounced as words or by letter, don't require them (NASA, GOP, OH).

Question marks. End a direct question with a question mark, but use a period to end an **indirect question**—a sentence with an embedded clause that asks a question.

DIRECT	When is the train leaving**?**
DIRECT: TWO CLAUSES	Considering that the tax break has been widely publicized, why have so few people filed for a refund**?**

DIRECT: QUOTED	Lu asked, "Why is it so hot**?**"
INDIRECT	Lu asked why it is so hot.

Exclamation points. These marks end emphatic statements such as commands or warnings but are rarely used in academic or work writing.

DRAFT	Rescuers spent hours (**!**) trying to reach the child.
EDITED	Rescuers spent **agonizing** hours trying to reach the child.

44g Recognizing and editing electronic addresses

When you cite an electronic address, record its characters exactly—including slashes, @ ("at") signs, underscores, colons, and periods.

http**:**//www**.**access**.**gpo**.**gov/su__docs

44h Combining marks

- **Always use marks that enclose in pairs.**

  ( )   [ ]   " "   ' '

  Use commas and dashes in pairs to enclose midsentence elements; use one pair of dashes at a time. Type a dash as a pair——of hyphens.

- **Use multiple marks when each mark plays its own role.** If an abbreviation with a period falls midsentence, the period may be followed by another mark, such as a comma, dash, colon, or semicolon.

  Experts spoke until 10 **p.m.,** and we left at 11 **p.m.**

- **Eliminate multiple marks when their roles overlap.** When an abbreviation with a period concludes a sentence, that one period will also end the sentence. Omit a comma *before* midsentence parentheses; *after* the parentheses, use whatever mark would otherwise occur.

- **Avoid confusing duplicates.** If items listed in a sentence include commas, separate them with semicolons, not more commas.

____ ,____ ,____ ; ____ ,____ ,____ ; and ____ .

If one parenthetical element falls within another, use brackets to enclose the unit inside the parentheses.

_____ (___ [___] ___).

SERIOUS ERROR

Ten Serious Errors

1. The heavy rain turned the parking lot to mud. **And stranded thousands of cars.**	**Fragment:** p. 226; Chapter 21
2. The promoters called **the insurance company they discovered** their coverage for accidents was limited.	**Fused Sentence:** p. 227; Chapter 22
3. After talking with the groundskeeper, the security chief said **he** would not be responsible for the safety of the crowd.	**Unclear Pronoun Reference:** p. 228; Chapter 23
4. Away from the microphone, the mayor said, "I hope the security chief or the promoters **has** a plan to help everyone leave safely."	**Lack of Subject-Verb Agreement:** p. 229; Chapter 24
5. **After announcing the cancellation from the stage, the crowd** began complaining to the promoters.	**Dangling Modifier:** p. 229; Chapter 28
6. If **people** left the arena quickly, **you** could get to **your** car without standing in the rain.	**Shift:** p. 230; Chapter 29
7. Even the **promoters promise** to reschedule and honor tickets did little to stop the **crowds' complaints.**	**Misused or Missing Apostrophe:** p. 230; Chapter 36
8. **Although,** the muddy lot caused problems, all the cars and **people, began** to leave.	**Unnecessary Commas:** p. 230; Chapter 34
9. "The grounds are **slippery, the** mayor repeated, "so please walk carefully."	**Missing or Misused Quotation Marks:** p. 221; Chapter 37
10. The authorities were relieved because they **hadn't scarcely** enough resources to cope.	**Double Negative:** p. 231; 25f

What happens when readers encounter a serious error in grammar, punctuation, or expression? They may stop paying attention to what you have to say and start looking through the passage for information to resolve any confusion or distraction created by the error. They may feel irritated over the time your error has wasted and think of you as careless or worse.

To identify the errors that readers consider most serious, we surveyed academics and professionals from varied fields. They identified these ten as most likely to create strong negative reactions from readers.

1. Fragment

Recognize. Some fragments lack a subject or verb. They force readers to hunt for a likely subject or verb in the passage or to supply one (see 21a, including tests for fragments).

NO SUBJECT   Rewrote the zero-tolerance policy. (Who did?)

NO VERB   The school board. (Did or is what?)

Other fragments begin with a subordinating word such as *though, while,* or *that* (see 31b). These words introduce a subordinate clause and force readers to attach the clause to a nearby sentence.

FRAGMENT   Because tea is increasingly popular. (Then what?)

Revise. Either provide the missing subject or verb, or attach the subordinate clause to a sentence it modifies.

The **school board rewrote** the zero-tolerance policy.

Because tea is increasingly popular, **coffee shops offer it.**

RECOGNIZING A SENTENCE

A **sentence**—also called **a main (or independent) clause**—is a word group that can stand alone. It has a subject and a predicate (a verb and any words that complete it).

SENTENCE   **Hungry bears** <u>were hunting</u> food in urban areas because spring snows had damaged many plants.

A **subordinate (or dependent) clause** has a subject and a predicate, yet it cannot stand on its own because it begins with a subordinating word such as *because, although, which*, or *that* (see 31b).

FRAGMENT   <u>Because</u> **spring snows** <u>had damaged</u> many plants

A **phrase** is a word group that lacks a subject, a predicate, or both, such as *were hunting, in urban areas*, or *the hungry bears*.

---

2. Fused Sentence

Recognize. Two sentences joined without a punctuation mark or connecting word create a **fused sentence.** Look for a series of word groups that could stand alone as sentences but do not use words (*and, but, however*, or *for example*) or punctuation (a semicolon or colon; see 22a–b) to tell readers where one sentence ends and the next begins.

FUSED   Revenue will grow profits will not increase.

REVISED   Revenue will grow, **but** profits will not increase.

Revise. Choose one of the five strategies illustrated in 22c.

1. Divide into two sentences.
2. Join with a comma plus *and, but, or, for, nor, so,* or *yet.*
3. Connect with a semicolon.
4. Subordinate one part with a word like *though* or *that* (see 31b).

5. Connect with an expression such as *however, moreover, in contrast,* or *for example* (see 31a) <u>plus</u> a semicolon.

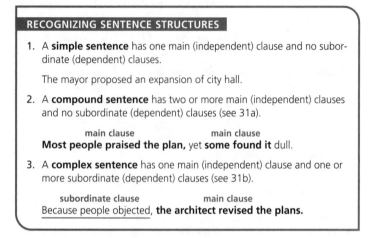

RECOGNIZING SENTENCE STRUCTURES

1. A **simple sentence** has one main (independent) clause and no subordinate (dependent) clauses.

   The mayor proposed an expansion of city hall.

2. A **compound sentence** has two or more main (independent) clauses and no subordinate (dependent) clauses (see 31a).

   main clause   main clause
   Most people praised the plan, yet **some found it** dull.

3. A **complex sentence** has one main (independent) clause and one or more subordinate (dependent) clauses (see 31b).

   subordinate clause   main clause
   <u>Because people objected</u>, **the architect revised the plans.**

3. Unclear Pronoun Reference

Recognize. A pronoun takes the place of a noun (or another pronoun) and makes sense to readers only if they can clearly recognize the word (**antecedent**) to which it refers.

        antecedent   pronoun
We installed **the tank,** but soon **it** started leaking.

Revise. Be sure that you state a pronoun's antecedent, place it nearby, and position it so that it is clear, not ambiguous (see 23b).

MISSING   After you turn on the fan, **it** will not be cool for an hour.

REVISED	After you turn on the fan, **the room** will not be cool for an hour.
AMBIGUOUS	Do not place the laptop near the router because **its** operation will be disrupted.
REVISED	Do not place the laptop near the router because **the laptop** will disrupt **its** operation.

4. Lack of Subject-Verb Agreement

Recognize. Subjects and verbs should match (or agree), both singular or both plural. Mismatched parts distract readers or force them to re-read.

      singular   singular
The **information** gathered by the team members **is** excellent.

Revise. Watch for a final -*s,* which often marks a plural subject but a singular verb. Look, too, for the *real* subject of a sentence (see 24b).

FAULTY	The cover [singular] resist [plural] dust.
REVISED	The cover **resists** dust.
FAULTY	The costs of an interactive program has grown.
REVISED	The **costs** of an interactive program **have** grown.

5. Dangling Modifier

Recognize. Readers expect an initial modifying phrase to name the person, thing, or idea it modifies or to modify the subject of the sentence. If it does neither, readers will wonder why it seems to modify something else (see 28a).

DANGLING	Covered with grease, the boys could not climb the pole.

Revise. To revise a dangling modifier, add the word or words modified.

REVISED   Covered with grease, **the pole** was too slippery for the boys to climb.

6. Shift

Recognize. When a sentence shifts pronouns or time frame illogically, readers may be confused or irritated.

PRONOUN SHIFT   **People** [they] create businesses from something **you** like to do.

TENSE SHIFT   Even though I **added** [past] the catalyst, nothing **happens** [present].

Revise. Stick to a logical perspective (*I, we, you, they,* and *he, she,* or *it;* 29a–b) or shift in time (see 29c–d).

REVISED   **People** create businesses from something **they** like to do.

REVISED   Even though I **added** the catalyst, nothing **happened.**

7. Misused or Missing Apostrophe

Recognize. Writing *it's* (= *it is*) for the possessive *its* or *sport's* for *sports* (more than one) forces readers to decide the meaning by themselves. Even when they can easily do so, they may be irritated by stray or missing apostrophes (see 36a–d).

Revise. Proofread your apostrophes. Check words that sometimes, but not always, include them (*girls, girl's, girls'; its, it's*).

8. Unnecessary Commas

Recognize. Commas appear often, but when too many fill a passage or too few join or set off sentence elements, readers may struggle to sort out ideas.

DISTRACTING   After, she had assembled the data, from her observations, Chris, reviewed the information, and decided, that she needed to do further research.

Revise. Instead of guessing where commas belong, learn the rules (34a–d, 34f), and edit with a reference like this handbook nearby.

REVISED   After she had assembled the data from her observations, Chris reviewed the information and decided that she needed to do further research.

9. Missing or Misused Quotation Marks

Recognize. Quotation marks distinguish what the writer says and what another person or a source has said. Because they identify the actual words of a source, quotation marks when misused create inaccuracies and confuse readers.

MISUSED   "The novel, Stephen Rose claims," "reflects the cultural conflicts caused by immigration, though this conclusion applies only to part of the work.

Revise. Quotation marks come in pairs (". . ."). Check for any that are missing (and thus don't acknowledge words from a source), that begin but don't end, or that enclose more than they should (see 37b, 44h).

REVISED   **"**The novel,**"** Stephen Rose claims, **"**reflects the cultural conflicts caused by immigration,**"** though this conclusion applies only to part of the work.

10. Double Negative

Recognize. Informally, double negatives can be forceful: "I'm not going, no way, no how!" They have the opposite effect in formal writing, where readers may view them as inappropriate or uneducated expressions—a harsh but likely judgment.

Revise. Stick to one negative. Avoid pairing words such as *no, none, not, never, hardly, scarcely,* and *don't.* (See 25f.)

DOUBLE   I have **scarcely no** data to support my conclusions.

REVISED   I have **scarcely any** data to support my conclusions.

Glossary of Usage and Terms

This glossary includes matters of usage (words that writers often find confusing or difficult, such as *farther* and *further*), grammatical terms (such as *verb*), and rhetorical terms (such as *indirect quotation*).

a, an Use *an* before a vowel (*an old film*) or silent *h* (*an honor*) and *a* before a consonant (*a classic, a hero*). (See pp. 170–71.)

accept, except *Accept* means "to take or receive"; *except* means "excluding."

Everyone **accepted** the invitation **except** Larry.

active voice (See **voice.**)

adverse, averse Someone opposed to something is *averse* to it; *adverse* conditions oppose achieving a goal.

advice, advise *Advice,* a noun, means "counsel" or "recommendations." *Advise,* a verb, means "to counsel or recommend."

He tried to **advise** students who wanted no **advice.**

affect, effect The verb *affect* means "to influence." *Effect* as a noun means "a result" and, rarely, as a verb means "to cause something to happen."

Because CFCs may **affect** the ozone layer with an uncertain **effect** on global warming, our goal is to **effect** changes in public attitudes.

aggravate, irritate *Aggravate* means "to worsen"; *irritate* means "to bother."

ain't Replace *ain't* in formal writing with *am not, is not,* or *are not.* The contractions *aren't* and *isn't* are more acceptable but are still informal.

all ready, already *All ready* means "prepared"; *already* means "by that time."

Sam was **all ready,** but the team had **already** gone.

all right Always spell this as two words, not as *alright.*

all together, altogether Use *all together* to mean "everyone"; use *altogether* to mean "completely."

allude, elude *Allude* means "refer indirectly"; *elude* means "escape."

allusion, illusion   An *allusion* is a reference to something; an *illusion* is a vision or false belief.

a lot   Even when spelled correctly as two words, not as *alot, a lot* may be too informal for some writing. Use *many* or *much* instead.

a.m., p.m.   These abbreviations may be capitals or lowercase (see 40a).

among, between   Use *between* when something involves two things; use *among* for three or more.

A fight **between** two players led to a debate **among** umpire and managers.

amount, number   *Amount* refers to a quantity of something that can't be divided into separate units; *number* refers to countable objects.

The recipe uses a **number** of spices and a small **amount** of milk.

an   (See **a, an.**)

and etc.   (See **etc.**)

and/or   Because *and/or* is imprecise, choose one of the words, or revise.

ante-, anti-   The prefix *ante-* means "before" or "predating," while *anti-* means "against" or "opposed."

antecedent   The noun or pronoun to which another word (usually a pronoun) refers (see Chapter 23).

anyone, any one   *Anyone* is an indefinite pronoun; you may also use *any* to modify *one,* in the sense of "any individual thing or person."

Anyone can dive, but the coach has little time for **any one** person.

anyplace   Replace this term in formal writing with *anywhere,* or revise.

anyways, anywheres   Avoid these versions of *anyway* and *anywhere.*

appositive   A noun or pronoun that renames or stands for a prior noun.

appositive phrase   An **appositive** (usually a noun) and its modifiers that rename or stand for a prior noun to add detail to a sentence.

Ken and Beth, **my classmates,** won an award.

as, like   Used as a preposition, *as* indicates a precise comparison. *Like* indicates a resemblance or similarity.

Remembered **as** a man of habit, Kant, **like** many other philosophers, was thoughtful and intense.

as to *As to* is considered informal in many contexts.

> INFORMAL   The media speculated **as to** the film's success.
>
> EDITED   The media speculated **about** the film's success.

assure, ensure, insure Use *assure* to imply a promise, *ensure* to imply a certain outcome, and *insure* to imply something legal or financial.

> The surgeon **assured** the pianist that his hands would heal by May. To **ensure** that, the musician **insured** his hands with Lloyd's of London.

at In writing, drop *at* in direct and indirect questions.

> SPOKEN   Jones asked where his attorney was **at.**
>
> EDITED   Jones asked where his attorney **was.**

awful, awfully Use *awful* (adjective) to modify a noun; use *awfully* (adverb) to modify a verb.

> He played **awfully** on that hole and sent an **awful** shot into the pond.

awhile, a while *Awhile* (one word) acts as an adverb; it is not preceded by a preposition. *A while* acts as a noun (with *a*) in prepositional phrases.

> The homeless family stayed **awhile** at the shelter because the children had not eaten for **a while.**

bad, badly Use *bad* (adjective) with a noun or linking verb expressing feelings, not the adverb *badly* (see 25f).

because, since Use *since* to indicate time, not causality in place of the more formal and precise *because*.

being as, being that Write *because* instead.

beside, besides Use *beside* to mean "next to." Use *besides* for "also" (adverb) or "except" (adjective).

> **Besides** being the firm's tax specialist, Klein would review nearly any document placed **beside** him.

better, had better Revise to *ought to* or *should* in formal writing.

between (See **among, between.**)

block quotation A quotation long enough to require separating it from the text in an indented block (see 16d).

bring, take *Bring* implies movement from somewhere else to close at hand; *take* implies the opposite direction.

Bring more coffee, but **take** away the muffins.

broke *Broke* is the past tense of *break,* not the past participle (see 25a).

| DRAFT | The computer was **broke.** |
| EDITED | The computer was **broken.** |

burst, bursted *Burst* implies an outward explosion: The boys *burst* the balloon. Do not use *bursted* for the past tense.

bust, busted Avoid *bust* or *busted* to mean "broke."

| COLLOQUIAL | The van **bust** down on the trip. |
| EDITED | The van **broke** down on the trip. |

but however, but yet Choose one word of each pair.

can, may *Can* implies ability; *may* implies permission or uncertainty.

Bart **can** drive, but his dad **may** not lend him the car.

can't hardly, can't scarcely Use these positively (*can hardly, can scarcely*), or simply use *can't* (see 25f).

capital, capitol *Capital* refers to a government center, a letter, or money; *capitol* refers to a government building.

censor, censure *Censor* means the act of shielding something from the public, such as a book. *Censure* implies punishment or critical labeling.

center around Use *center on, focus on,* or *revolve around.*

choose, chose Use *choose* for the present and *chose* for the past tense.

cite, site *Cite* means to acknowledge someone's work; *site* means a place.

Phil **cited** field studies of the Anasazi **site.**

clause A word group with a subject and a verb. A **main** (independent) clause can stand on its own; a **subordinate** (dependent) clause begins with a subordinating word (*because, although, that*) and cannot stand alone (see 31b).

Because he lost his balance, Sam fell on the ice.

climactic, climatic *Climactic* refers to the culmination of something; *climatic* refers to weather conditions.

comma splice Two or more sentences (main clauses) incorrectly joined with a comma. (See 22a, c.)

comparative The form of an adjective or adverb showing that the word it modifies is compared to one other thing (see 25g). The comparative form adds *-er* or *more* (*faster, more adept*). (See **superlative.**)

compare to, compare with Use *compare to* and *liken to* for similarities between two things. Use *compare with* for both similarities and differences.

> **Compared with** the boy's last illness, this virus, which the doctor **compared to** a tiny army, was mild.

complement A word (noun, pronoun, adjective) or phrase tied to a subject by a **linking verb** (*becomes, is, seems*). A **subject complement** describes or renames a subject: Nan seems **tired.** An **object complement** does the same for a direct object: Brad ate the pizza **cold.**

complement, compliment *Complement* means "an accompaniment"; *compliment* means "words of praise."

> The guests **complimented** the chef on the menu, which **complemented** the event perfectly.

compound modifier Two or more words that work as a single modifier (**woodburning** *fireplace*).

compound object Two or more objects joined by *and* or *both . . . and.*

compound subject Two or more subjects joined by *and* or *both . . . and.*

compound word A word made up of two or more independent words (such as *superman* or *father-in-law*).

conjunction A word that joins two elements in a sentence. **Coordinating conjunctions** (*and, but, or, nor, for, yet, so*) link grammatically equal elements—compound subjects, verbs, objects, and modifiers. **Subordinating conjunctions** (*because, although, while, if*) create a subordinate clause. (See 31a–b.)

conjunctive adverb An adverb (*however, moreover, therefore*) that joins sentences or sentence elements, showing how they are related (see 31a).

continual, continuous *Continual* implies that something recurs; *continuous* implies that it is constant or unceasing.

The **continual** noise of the jets was less annoying than the traffic **continuously** circling the airport.

coordinate adjectives Two adjectives, each modifying a noun on its own, separated by a comma. If the first modifies the second (which modifies the noun), they are **noncoordinate adjectives,** not separated by a comma.

coordinating conjunction One of seven words (*and, but, or, nor, for, yet, so*) that link equal elements (see 31a). (See **conjunction.**)

coordination A sentence structure using **coordinating conjunctions** to link and weight main clauses equally (see 31a, c).

could of, would of Replace these, often pronounced as they are misspelled, with *could have* or *would have*.

couple, couple of In formal writing, use *a few* or *two*.

criteria *Criteria* is the plural form of *criterion*.

> PLURAL   The **criteria** were too strict to follow.

curriculum *Curriculum* is the singular form. For the plural, use either *curricula* or *curriculums* consistently.

dangling modifier (See **misplaced modifier.**)

data Widely used for both singular and plural, *data* technically is plural; *datum* refers to a single piece of data. If in doubt, use the plural.

> PLURAL   These **data** are not very revealing.

different from, different than Use *different from* when an object follows; use *different than* (not *from what*) when a clause follows.

> Jim's tacos are **different from** Lena's; his enchiladas now are **different than** they were when he began to cook.

direct quotation A statement that repeats someone's exact words, set off by quotation marks (see 37b). (See also **indirect quotation.**)

discreet, discrete *Discreet* means "reserved or cautious"; *discrete* means "distinctive" or "explicit."

disinterested, uninterested *Disinterested* implies impartiality or objectivity; *uninterested* implies lack of interest.

disruptive modifier (See **misplaced modifier.**)

done *Done* is a past participle, not past tense (see 25a).

   DRAFT   The runner **done** her best at the meet.
   EDITED   The runner **did** her best at the meet.

don't, doesn't Contractions may be too informal in some contexts. Ask your reader, or err on the side of formality (*do not, does not*).

double negative Avoid double negatives (see 25f).

   DRAFT   The state **hasn't** done **nothing** about it.
   EDITED   The state **has** done **nothing** about it.
   EDITED   The state **hasn't** done **anything** about it.

due to To mean "because," use *due to* only after a form of the verb *be*. Avoid the wordy *due to the fact that*.

   DRAFT   The mayor collapsed **due to** fatigue.
   EDITED   The mayor's collapse was **due to** fatigue.
   EDITED   The mayor collapsed **because** of fatigue.

effect, affect (See **affect, effect**.)

e.g. Avoid this abbreviation meaning "for example."

   AWKWARD   Her positions on issues, **e.g.,** gun control, are very liberal.
   EDITED   Her positions on issues **such as** gun control are very liberal.

ellipsis A series of three spaced periods showing a reader where something has been left out of a quotation (see 44d).

emigrate from, immigrate to People *emigrate from* one country and *immigrate to* another. *Migrate* implies moving about (*migrant workers*) or settling temporarily.

ensure (See **assure, ensure, insure**.)

enthused Avoid *enthused* for *enthusiastic* in writing.

especially, specially *Especially* implies "in particular"; *specially* means "for a specific purpose."

   It was **especially** important to follow the **specially** designed workouts.

etc. Avoid this abbreviation in formal writing; supply a complete list, or use a phrase like *so forth*.

INFORMAL	The march was a disaster: it rained, the protesters had no food, **etc.**
EDITED	The march was a disaster: the protesters were wet and hungry.

eventually, ultimately Use *eventually* for an outcome after a series (or lapse) of events; use *ultimately* for a final act ending a series of events.

Eventually, the rescuers pulled the last victim from the wreck, and **ultimately** there were no casualties.

everyday, every day *Everyday* (adjective) modifies a noun. *Every day* is a noun (*day*) modified by *every*.

Every day in the Peace Corps, Monique faced the **everyday** task of boiling her drinking water.

everyone, every one *Everyone* is a pronoun; *every one* is an adjective followed by a noun.

Everyone was dazzled by **every one** of the desserts.

exam In formal writing, readers may prefer the full term, *examination*.

except (See **accept, except.**)

expletive construction Opening with *there is, there are,* or *it is* to delay the subject until later in the sentence (see 26b).

explicit, implicit *Explicit* means that something is openly stated, *implicit* that it is implied or suggested.

farther, further *Farther* implies a distance that can be measured; *further* implies one that cannot.

The **farther** they hiked, the **further** their friendship deteriorated.

faulty predication A sentence flaw in which the second part (the predicate) comments on a topic different from the one in the first part (see 27a–b).

FAULTY	The **presence** of ozone in smog is the **chemical** that causes eye irritation.
EDITED	The **ozone** in smog is the **chemical** that causes eye irritation.

female, male Use these terms only to specify gender, as in a research report. Otherwise, use *man* or *woman* unless such usage is sexist (see 33b).

fewer, less Use *fewer* for things that can be counted, and use *less* for quantities that cannot be divided.

The new bill had **fewer** supporters and **less** media coverage.

first person Pronouns (*I, we*) for the person speaking. (See **person.**)

firstly Use *first, second, third* when enumerating points.

form The spelling or ending that shows a word's role in a sentence. (See Chapter 25.)

former, latter *Former* means "the one before" and *latter* means "the one after." The pair must refer to only two things.

fragment Part of a sentence incorrectly treated as complete. (See 21a–b.)

freshman, freshmen Readers may consider these terms sexist. Except for established terms (such as Freshman Colloquium), use *first-year student.*

fused sentence Two or more complete sentences incorrectly joined without any punctuation; also called a **run-on sentence.** (See 22b, c.)

genre The form or type of text to which a work conforms (play, novel, lab report, essay, memo).

get Replace this word with more specific verbs.

INFORMAL	King's last speeches **got** nostalgic.
EDITED	King's last speeches **turned** nostalgic.

go, say Some speakers use *go* and *goes* very informally for *say* and *says.* Revise this usage in all writing.

gone, went Do not use *went* (past tense of *go*) for the past participle form *gone.*

DRAFT	The officers **should have went** to the captain.
EDITED	The officers **should have gone** to the captain.

good and In formal writing, avoid this term to mean "very" (*good and* tired).

good, well *Good* (an adjective) means "favorable" (a *good* trip). *Well* (an adverb) means "done favorably." Avoid informal uses of *good* for *well.*

got to Avoid *got* or *got to* in place of *must* or *have to.*

SPOKEN	I **got to** improve my grade in statistics.
WRITTEN	I **have to** improve my grade in statistics.

great Formally, avoid *great* as an adjective meaning "wonderful"; use it to mean "large" or "monumental."

hanged, hung Some readers will expect you to use *hanged* exclusively to mean execution by hanging and *hung* to refer to anything else.

have, got (See **got to**.)

have, of (See **could of, would of**.)

he, she Avoid privileging male forms (see 33b).

helping verb A form of a verb such as *be, do,* or *have* that can be combined with a main verb (see 25a).

hopefully Some readers may object when this word modifies an entire clause ("*Hopefully, her health will improve*"). When in doubt, use it only as "feeling hopeful."

however (See **but however, but yet**.)

hung (See **hanged, hung**.)

if, whether Use *if* before a specific outcome (stated or implied); use *whether* to consider alternatives.

If the technology can be perfected, we may soon have three-dimensional television. But **whether** we will be able to afford it is another question.

illogical comparison (See **incomplete sentence**.)

illusion (See **allusion, illusion**.)

immigrate to (See **emigrate from, immigrate to**.)

implicit (See **explicit, implicit**.)

incomplete comparison (See **incomplete sentence**.)

incomplete sentence A sentence that fails to complete an expected logical or grammatical pattern. An **incomplete comparison** leaves out the element to which something is compared; an **illogical comparison** seems to compare things that cannot be reasonably compared. (See Chapter 27.)

independent clause (See **main clause**.)

indirect question A sentence whose main clause is a statement and whose embedded clause asks a question. Treat these as statements, not questions.

Phil wondered **what the study would show.**

indirect quotation A quotation in which a writer reports the substance of someone's words but not the exact words used. Quotation marks are not needed. (See **direct quotation;** see Chapter 37.)

in regard to Replace this wordy phrase with *about*.

inside of, outside of When you use *inside* or *outside* to mark locations, omit *of*: *Inside* the hut was a child.

insure (See **assure, ensure, insure.**)

interpolation Your own words, marked with brackets, introduced into a direct quotation from someone else (see 44c).

interrupter A parenthetical remark such as *in fact* or *more importantly*.

irregardless Avoid this erroneous form of *regardless*.

irritate (See **aggravate, irritate.**)

its, it's *Its* is a possessive pronoun; *it's* is a contraction for *it is*. (See Chapter 36.) Some readers object to contractions in formal writing.

-ize, -wise Some readers object to turning nouns or adjectives into verbs by adding *-ize* (*finalize, itemize, computerize*). Avoid adding *-wise* to words: "Weather-*wise*, it's chilly."

keyword A word in a database, catalog, or index used to identify a topic.

kind, sort, type Precede these singular nouns with *this*, not *these*. In general, use more precise words.

kind of, sort of Avoid these informal expressions (meaning "a little," "rather," or "somewhat") in academic and workplace writing.

latter (See **former, latter.**)

lay, lie Use *lay* to place an object and *lie* to position the self (see 25a).

less (See **fewer, less.**)

lie (See **lay, lie.**)

like (See **as, like.**)

limiting modifier A word such as *only, almost,* or *just* that qualifies a word, usually the one that follows it. (See 28a.)

linking verb A verb that expresses a state of being or an occurrence: *is, seems, becomes, grows*.

literally In both factual and figurative (not true to fact) statements, avoid *literally*.

DRAFT	Jed **literally** died when he saw the hotel.
REDUNDANT	Jed **literally gasped** when he saw the hotel.
EDITED	Jed **gasped** when he saw the hotel.

loose, lose *Loose* (rhyming with *moose*) is an adjective meaning "not tight." *Lose* (rhyming with *snooze*) is a present tense verb meaning "to misplace."

lots (See **a lot.**)

main clause A word group with a subject and a verb that can stand on its own as a sentence. (See **clause.**)

may (See **can, may.**)

maybe, may be *Maybe* means *possibly; may be* is part of a verb structure.

The President **may be** speaking now, so **maybe** we should listen.

media, medium Technically plural, *media* is often used as a singular noun to refer to the press. *Medium* generally refers to a method of transmission.

The **media** is not covering the story accurately.

The telephone is a useful **medium** for planning.

might of (See **could of, would of.**)

mighty In formal writing, omit or replace *mighty* with *very*.

misplaced modifier A modifier incorrectly placed relative to the word it modifies (its headword). (See Chapter 28.)

mixed sentence A sentence with a mismatched or shifted grammatical structure. (See Chapter 27.)

modifier A word or word group, acting as an adjective or adverb, that qualifies the meaning of another word (see 25e–f).

modify The function of adjectives and adverbs that add to, qualify, limit, or extend the meaning of other words.

Ms. To avoid sexist labeling of women by marital status (not marked in men's titles), use *Ms.* unless you have reason to use *Miss* or *Mrs.* (as in the name of the character *Mrs. Dalloway*). Use professional titles when appropriate (*Dr., Professor, Senator, Mayor*).

must of, must have (See **could of, would of.**)

nominalization A noun (*modernization, verbosity*) created from a verb (*modernize*) or adjective (*verbose*). (See 26b.)

noncoordinate adjectives (See **coordinate adjectives.**)

nonrestrictive modifier (See **restrictive modifier.**)

nor, or Use *nor* for negative and *or* for positive constructions.

NEGATIVE	Neither rain **nor** snow will slow the team.
POSITIVE	Either rain **or** snow may delay the game.

nothing like, nowhere near In formal writing, avoid these informal phrases used to compare two things.

noun string A sequence of nouns used to modify a main noun (*multifunction modulation control device*) that may seem abstract or technical to readers.

nowheres Use *nowhere* instead.

number The way of showing whether a noun or pronoun is **singular** (one) or **plural** (two or more). Subjects and verbs must agree in number, as must pronouns and the nouns they modify. (See Chapter 24 and 29a–b; see also **amount, number.**)

object The words in a sentence that tell who or what receives the action.

The class cleaned up **the park.**

of, have (See **could of, would of.**)

off of Use *off* instead.

OK When you write formally, use *OK* only in dialogue. If you mean "good" or "acceptable," use these terms.

on account of In formal writing, use *because*.

outside of (See **inside of, outside of.**)

parallelism The expression of similar or related ideas in similar grammatical form (see Chapter 30).

paraphrase To rewrite a passage in your own words, preserving the essence and detail of the original (see 14b).

passive voice (See **voice.**)

per Use *per* to mean "by the," as in *per hour,* not "according to," as in *per your instructions.*

percent, percentage Use *percent* with numbers (*10 percent*); use *percentage* for a statistical part of something (*a large percentage of the budget*).

person The form that a noun or pronoun takes to identify the subject of a sentence. **First person** is someone speaking (*I, we*); **second person** is someone spoken to (*you*); **third person** is someone being spoken about (*he, she, it, they*). (See Chapter 24 and 29a–b.)

personal pronoun A pronoun that designates persons or things, such *as I, me, you, him, we, you, they.* (See 25c–d.)

phrase A word group without a subject, a verb, or both. (See **clause.**)

plagiarism The unethical or illegal practice of using another writer's words or text as your own without acknowledging their source (see 16a).

plus Use *and* to join two main clauses. Use *plus* only to mean "in addition to."

possessive A pronoun (*mine, hers, yours, theirs*) or noun (*the **bird's** egg*) that expresses ownership. (See 25c and 36a–b.)

precede, proceed *Precede* means "come before"; *proceed* means "go ahead."

predicate The words in a sentence that indicate an action, relationship, or condition—typically a **verb phrase** following the subject of the sentence. A **simple predicate** is a verb or verb phrase; to these, a **complete predicate** adds modifiers or other words that receive action or complete the verb.

prefix An addition, such as *un-* in *unforgiving*, at the beginning of a word. (See **suffix.**)

pretty Use *pretty* to mean "attractive," not "somewhat" or "rather" (as in *pretty good, pretty hungry*).

primary source Research material in or close to original form (see p. 45).

principal, principle Principal is a noun meaning "an authority" or "head of a school" or an adjective meaning "leading" ("*a principal* objection to the testimony"). *Principle* is a noun meaning "belief or conviction."

proceed (See **precede, proceed.**)

quote, quotation Formally, *quote* is a verb, and *quotation* is a noun. Some readers object to *quote* as an abbreviation of *quotation*.

raise, rise *Raise* is a transitive verb meaning "to lift up." *Rise* is an intransitive verb (it takes no object) meaning "to get up or move up."

He **raised** his head to watch the sun **rise.**

rarely ever Use *rarely* alone, not paired with *ever*.

real, really Use *real* as an adjective; use *really* as an adverb (see 25f).

reason is because, reason is that Avoid these wordy phrases (see 27b).

redundancy The use of unnecessary or repeated words (see 32a).

regarding (See **in regard to.**)

regardless (See **irregardless.**)

relative clause A clause that modifies a noun or pronoun and begins with a **relative pronoun** (*who, whom, whose, which, that*).

Jen found a Web site **that** had valuable links.

respectfully, respectively Use *respectfully* for "with respect" and *respectively* to imply an order or sequence.

The senate **respectfully** submitted revisions for items 4 and 10, **respectively.**

restrictive modifier A **restrictive modifier** supplies information essential to the meaning of a sentence and is added without commas. A **nonrestrictive modifier** adds useful or interesting information not essential to the meaning and is set off by commas (see 34d).

rise (See **raise, rise.**)

run-on sentence (See **fused sentence.**)

says (See **go, say.**)

second person The pronoun (you) referring to the person spoken to. (See **person.**)

secondary source Research information that analyzes, interprets, or comments on primary sources (see p. 45). (See also **primary source.**)

sentence A group of words with both a subject and a complete verb that can stand on its own. (See **comma splice, fragment, fused sentence;** see p. 227, 21a, and Chapter 22.)

sentence cluster A group of sentences that develop related ideas or information.

set, sit *Set* means "to place"; *sit* means "to place oneself" (see 25a).

should of (See **could of, would of.**)

shift An inappropriate switch in **person, number, tense,** or topic. (See Chapter 29.)

since (See **because, since.**)

sit (See **set, sit.**)

site (See **cite, site.**)

so Some readers object to the use of *so* in place of *very*.

somebody, some body (See **anyone, any one.**)

someone, some one (See **anyone, any one.**)

sometime, some time, sometimes *Sometime* refers to a vague future time; *sometimes* means "every once in a while." *Some time* is an adjective (*some*) modifying a noun (*time*).

> **Sometime** every winter, **sometimes** after a project is finished, the crew takes **some time** off.

sort (See **kind, sort.**)

specially (See **especially, specially.**)

split infinitive An infinitive is the base form of a verb paired with *to* (to run). Some readers object to another word placed between the two (to **quickly** run). (See 28a.)

squinting modifier (See **misplaced modifier.**)

stationary, stationery *Stationary* means "standing still"; *stationery* refers to writing paper.

subject In a sentence, the doer or thing talked about, typically placed before a verb phrase. A **simple subject** consists of one or more nouns (or pronouns) naming the doer; to this a **complete subject** adds modifiers.

subject complement (See **complement.**)

subordinate clause A word group with a subject and a verb that is introduced by a subordinator (*because, although, that, which*). It must be connected to a main clause (which can stand alone). (See **clause;** see 31b–c.)

subordinating conjunction A word (*because, although, while, if*) that introduces a subordinate clause, a word group with a subject and verb that cannot stand alone and must be connected to a main clause. (See **conjunction;** see 31b.)

such Some readers will expect *that* to follow *such*.

> The team solved **such** a complex problem **that** everyone cheered.

suffix An addition, such as *-ly* in *quickly,* at the end of a word. (See **prefix.**)

summary A concise restatement in your own words, boiling a passage or source down to essentials (see 14a).

superlative The form of an adjective or adverb showing that the word it modifies is compared to two or more other things (see 25g). The superlative adds *-est* or *most* (*fastest, most adept*). (See **comparative.**)

suppose to Use the correct form, *supposed to,* even though the *-d* is not always heard in pronunciation. (See p. 160.)

sure, surely Formally, use *sure* to mean "certain." Use *surely,* not *sure,* as an adverb (see 25f).

He has **surely** studied hard and is **sure** to pass.

sure and, try and Write *sure to* and *try to* instead.

synthesis The distilling of separate elements into a single, unified entity. For a research paper, an analytical synthesis relates summaries of several sources while a critical synthesis presents conclusions about a variety of perspectives, opinions, or interpretations (see 14c).

take (See **bring, take.**)

tense The form a verb takes to indicate time—past, present, or future tense (see 25a–b).

than, then *Than* is used to compare; *then* implies a sequence of events.

Lil played harder **than** Eva; **then** the rain began.

that, which In formal writing, use *that* when a clause is essential to the meaning of a sentence (restrictive modifier) and *which* when it does not provide essential information (nonrestrictive modifier) (see 34d).

theirself, theirselves, themself Replace these with *themselves* to refer to more than one person and *himself* or *herself* to refer to one person.

them Avoid *them* as a subject or to modify a subject, as in "Them are fresh" or "Them apples are crisp." Replace with *they, these, those,* or *the* with a noun (*the apples*).

then (See **than, then.**)

there, their, they're These forms sound alike, but *there* shows location, *their* is a possessive pronoun, and *they're* contracts *they* and *are.*

Look over **there. Their** car ran out of gas. **They're** starting to walk.

third person Pronouns (*he, she, it, they*) that indicate the person or thing spoken about. (See **person;** see 29a–b.)

thusly Replace this term with *thus* or *therefore.*

till, until, 'til Some readers will find *'til* and *till* informal; use *until.*

to, too, two These words sound alike, but *to* is a preposition showing direction, *too* means "also," and *two* is a number.

Ed went **to** the lake **two** times and took Han **too.**

toward, towards Prefer *toward* in formal writing.

transitional expression Expressions (*therefore, in addition*) that link one idea, sentence, or paragraph to the next, helping readers relate ideas.

try and, try to (See **sure and, try and.**)

ultimately (See **eventually, ultimately.**)

uninterested (See **disinterested, uninterested.**)

unique Use *unique,* not *most* or *more unique* (see 25g).

until (See **till, until, 'til.**)

use to, used to Write *used to,* even though the *-d* is not always clearly pronounced. (See p. 160.)

verb The word in a sentence that expresses action (*jump*), occurrence (*happen*), or state of being (*be*). (See 25a.)

voice A verb is in the **active voice** when the doer of the action is the subject of the sentence and in the **passive voice** when the goal or object of the sentence is the subject. (See p. 165.)

wait for, wait on Use *wait on* for a clerk's or server's job; use *wait for* to mean "to await someone's arrival."

well (See **good, well.**)

went (See **gone, went.**)

were, we're *Were* is a verb; *we're* is a contraction for "we are."

where . . . at (See **at.**)

whether (See **if, whether.**)

which (See **that, which.**)

who, whom Though the distinction between these words is disappearing, many readers will expect the formal *whom* for an object (see 25d).

who's, whose *Who's* is a contraction for "who is"; *whose* shows possession.

-wise (See **-ize, -wise.**)

would of (See **could of, would of.**)

yet (See **but however, but yet.**)

your, you're *Your* is a possessive pronoun; *you're* contracts "you are."

If **you're** taking math, you'll need **your** calculator.

Index

Guide to ESL Advice

Look for the ESL Advice if your first language is not English. This advice is integrated throughout the handbook and highlighted so it's easy to spot.

Credits *(continued from p. vi)*

Synergy online database for article "A Queen for Whose Time? Elizabeth I as Icon for The Twentieth Century" by David Grant, *Journal of Popular Culture*, 39 (2006). By permission of Blackwell Publishing. **Page 93:** Screen shot of search results in pdf format from Blackwell Synergy online database for article "A Queen for Whose Time? Elizabeth I as Icon for The Twentieth Century" by David Grant, *Journal of Popular Culture*, 39 (2006). By permission of Blackwell Publishing. **Page 102:** Sadeh, Avi, Amiram Raviv, & Reut Gruber, "Sleep Patterns & Sleep Disruptions in School-Age Children," *Developmental Psychology*, Vol. 36, No. 3, May 2000. **Page 103:** Schor, Juliet B., *The Overworked American*. New York, NY: HarperCollins, 1998. **Page 117:** Screen shot for search result, "Treatment Approaches for Sleep Difficulties in College Students" from EBSCOhost *Academic Search Premier* online database. Reprinted by permission of EBSCO Publishing. Excerpt for "Treatment Approaches for Sleep Difficulties among College Students," by Walter C. Buboltz from *Counselling Psychology Quarterly*, September 2002, Vol. 15, No. 2. Reprinted by permission of the publisher, Taylor & Francis, Ltd. **Page 123:** Wideman, John Edgar, *Brothers and Keepers*. New York, NY: Random House, 1984. **Page 137:** Boutron, Claude F., et al., "Decrease in Anthropologic Lead, Cadmium and Zinc in Greenland Snows since the Late 1960's," *Nature*, Vol. 353, 1991. **Page 145:** Didion, Joan, "Why I Write," *New York Times Magazine*, December 5, 1976. Copyright 1976 by Joan Didion & The New York Times Company. **Page 173:** Mark Twain, from a letter to George Bainton, October 1888. **Page 193:** Visco, Frank L., *How to Write Good*. **Page 206:** Goddio, Frank, "San Diego: An Account of Adventure, Deceit and Intrigue," *National Geographic*, 1994. **Page 210:** Daseler, Robert, excerpt from "At the Barrier," *Levering Avenue Poems*. Evansville, IN: University of Evansville Press, 1998. **Page 222:** Sydney, Sir Philip, "His Lady's Cruelty," *The Oxford Book of English Verse 1250–1918*. London, UK: Oxford University Press, 1973. **Student Acknowledgments:** Summer Arrigo-Nelson, Anne Bloomfield, Pamela Copass, Kimlee Cunningham, Jennifer Figliozzi, Daisy Garcia, Tammy Jo Helton, Jenny Latimer, Sharon Salamone.

Contents